T0326606

Ideas and Innovative Organizations

This book is part of the Peter Lang Political Science, Economics, and Law list.
Every volume is peer reviewed and meets the highest quality
standards for content and production.

PETER LANG
New York • Bern • Berlin
Brussels • Vienna • Oxford • Warsaw

Albert H. Segars

Ideas and Innovative Organizations

A Tribal Perspective

PETER LANG
New York • Bern • Berlin
Brussels • Vienna • Oxford • Warsaw

Library of Congress Cataloging-in-Publication Data
Names: Segars, Albert H., author.
Title: Ideas and innovative organizations: a tribal perspective /
Albert H. Segars.
Description: 1 Edition. | New York: Peter Lang Publishing, Inc., 2020.
Includes bibliographical references.
Identifiers: LCCN 2019038036 | ISBN 978-1-4331-7464-3 (hardback: alk. paper)
ISBN 978-1-4331-7461-2 (ebook pdf)
ISBN 978-1-4331-7462-9 (epub) | ISBN 978-1-4331-7463-6 (mobi)
Subjects: LCSH: Organizational change. | Management—Technological
innovations. | Leadership.
Classification: LCC HD58.5 .S44 2020 | DDC 658.4/06—dc23
LC record available at https://lccn.loc.gov/2019038036
DOI 10.3726/b16442

Bibliographic information published by **Die Deutsche Nationalbibliothek**.
Die Deutsche Nationalbibliothek lists this publication in the "Deutsche
Nationalbibliografie"; detailed bibliographic data are available
on the Internet at http://dnb.d-nb.de/.

This work is dedicated to my extraordinary tribe. My wife Barbara Patton Segars and my children, Kristen Leigh Segars and Joseph Keith Segars.

CONTENTS

FIGURES

INTRODUCTION

Home is a place where, when you go there, they have to take you in

— Robert Frost

I have always wanted to be on the solution side of the equation. Therefore, I chose to be a scientist and embark on a career of exploration and discovery. I think this path found its seeding in the Apollo space exploration program of the 1970s. This program and its ambitious goal of landing humans on the moon found its way into my imagination and, for many elementary school kids growing up in the 1970s, became an embodiment of "magic" through creativity, engineering, science, and big ideas. For a moment in time, there were bigger ambitions, worlds to explore, and an army of wide-eyed dreamers ready to apply their talents to solving complex problems. Throughout history, times like these come and go based on cycles of technological innovation, generational trends, and the "give and take" of societal needs. There are periods of technological revolution which usher in dynamic change as well as periods of "in between" where change is more incremental.

Through several research projects, consulting engagements, and first-hand experience. I have enjoyed access to labs, think tanks, start-ups, as well as "skunk works" within established organizations that are investigating, developing, and converting cutting-edge technologies into viable products and services.[1] The ideas, discoveries, and breakthroughs observed from these organizations are incredible; in many respects, their efforts are the "tip of the spear" in terms of pioneering new frontiers. Therefore, understanding "why" they routinely discover new ideas and how they turn them into new avenues of value is to learn from the most "innovative of the innovative". It is also a chance to rediscover some of the big thinking and innovative work that chronicles not only a program like Apollo but any innovative effort that results in a breakthrough idea.

That is the purpose of this book: to describe the salient aspects of how an innovative group or organization "works" in terms of ambition, values, beliefs, and drive as well as associated tools and techniques that are used to uncover breakthrough ideas. What I have found is a way of working and a modality of innovation that have not been clearly or adequately described in books, articles or seminars. What I have seen and experienced in these groups and their organizations is "tribal". There is something that connects them with one another and something that connects them with their purpose that is more than the typical structure of a team. These tribes crave hardship, relish difficult tasks, value initiative, and are guided by thoughtful consensus. This approach has some familiar aspects of "work", but it is largely at direct odds with many principles of management and leadership.[2] I believe this tribal perspective is the leading indicator of modern leadership and has stark implications as to how problems are framed, how people engage, and what approach is used to drive results. It is the same "something" that explains the longevity of rock bands such as the Rolling Stones, the unprecedented run of super bowl titles by the New England Patriots, and the effectiveness of the Civil Rights Movement led by Dr. Martin Luther King. Yet, it is being applied today in very innovative organizations as they build new modes of commerce, new forms of manufacturing, and new approaches to healthcare. Importantly, innovation is a very broad frontier. It is not just developing new products, a new marketing campaign, or creating the new strategic strike. It is also developing programs of diversity and inclusiveness, creating better workplaces, partnering with the community, building benefits and compensation plans, and creating organizations that coexist with the earth's natural resources of land, air, and water. These and other important initiatives are sometimes framed as something different than innovation. It is a mistake. The most innovative organizations approach these challenges with the same vigor and same intensity as creating the next big product.

Importantly, a tribal perspective has deep historical roots and unlocks a cultural and less salient aspect of how something "more than ordinary" is accomplished. It speaks to the very heart of that "something" that separates an ordinary effort from an extraordinary accomplishment. It also reconciles how true innovation occurred in the past with how innovative organizations are reshaping technology and life today. For you and me, it is a way of thinking more tribally about the challenges we face and the frontiers we explore. It is also a way to instill tribal instincts in the people we lead, the teams we are on, or the tribes we are trying to unite. This is more than a typical book about business or management; it is about a person, a group of people, a super project, or an organization that has struck a form of harmony or connectedness in chasing something bigger than themselves. Such harmony can be found in a family, an athletic team, a social cause, a school, a church, a book club, a government agency, or a modern business. However, to find it, we must identify it. Being tribal is likely something we have all experienced at some point in our lifetime; it is time to rediscover it, embrace it, and put it to work in the name of real innovation. My hope is that the perspective helps you "Find Your Tribal Spirit" and leads you to a path to discover things beyond the ordinary.

Notes

1. Albert Segars, "Seven Technologies that Are Remaking the World," *Sloan Management Review*, March 2018.
2. D. Cable, *Alive at Work: The Neuroscience of Helping Your People Love What They Do*. Harvard Business Review Press, 2018.

· 1 ·

TRIBES, TRIBALISM, AND TRIBAL INSTINCTS

We're a melting pot of astronomers, physicists, mathematicians and engineers, and that's what it took to achieve something once thought impossible.
— Dr. Katie Bouman, Event Horizon Telescope, on capturing the first image of a black hole.

Perhaps all of us, at one time or another, have asked the question "How did they do that?" It may have been at the end of a magician's "illusion", after a fantastic athletic feat, or at the conclusion of a perfect performance of a difficult song. We often experience the fantastic as an observer. In doing so, we marvel at the feat of an athlete, the skill of the performer, the genius of the artist, or the ideas of the inventor. However, there are also moments in our lives when we are part of the fantastic; we win the game when all odds were stacked against our team, we complete the impossible project on time and within budget, we survive a scare when we were sure that the worst would happen, or we walk through a crisis when all seemed lost. In some respects, these moments, good and bad, are the "times of our lives". It is also a time when you are connected to a group of people and a task that is, in a way, "tribal". There is loyalty, a code of conduct, and a sense of purpose that transcends the normal rules of work or societal etiquette. It is a feeling of unique and important identity as you take on a quest. You are willing to give all you can to support those who are with you and to see the journey to its triumphant conclusion. In French, this common spirit of enthusiasm and devotion is captured in a powerful phrase, *Esprit de Corps*. This "something" is an important concept in explaining how fantastic accomplishments happen and what drives organizations and people to attempt what seems to be impossible. More than likely, we have all experienced or witnessed a tribal accomplishment at some point in our lifetime; perhaps now is the right time to understand it, harness it, and put it to work in our professional and personal lives. It certainly seems to be the extra ingredient and approach of forward-thinking organizations, inventors, and idea makers. To build a frame for exploring how a tribal approach works, let's look at tribes and their lofty accomplishments.

Tribes and Tribalism

To understand the concept of a "tribe" and "tribalism", it is important to look beyond a name, a uniform, a place, an ethnic group, an accent, or other visible indicators. It is not republican versus democrat, northern versus southern, or believer versus non-believer. Instead, it is a system of connectedness and shared purpose to achieve something beyond the ordinary. That is not to say that such connectedness and accomplishment cannot be found in tribes that are readily identifiable. Native American tribes such as the Cherokee and Navajo pioneered many important principles of ecology, conservation, and farming. Egyptian and Viking tribes were the inventors of ship building and navigational technology that is still used today. Beyond the common bond of place and genetics, tribes such as these have as their core a strong connection among members, an ambitious cause, and a responsibility to look out for one another in all circumstances. In the extreme case, tribal members are even willing to fight and die for one another. While today's context of innovation is not one of human survival and no one is asked to sacrifice his or her life for another, there are very identifiable attributes of tribalism that are found among innovative groups that are not found in typical organizational teams.

Ironically, many organizations have well-established structures that vanquish tribal spirit. Other organizations may have had a tribal mentality but then grew their way out of it. Given that a core need of ambitious people is to feel necessary and feel part of something bigger than themselves, it is no wonder that some feel unsatisfied or even unnecessary in traditional organizations. In a recent survey, it was discovered that executives and scientists between the ages of 25 and 40 years identified more strongly with their work groups than the organizations they work for.[1] Such a finding challenges many traditional assumptions of how and why people perform within their jobs. Among the millennial generation, social networking in and out of the digital realm is a readily identifiable trait. This phenomenon has rapidly spread to generations before and after the millennials. Perhaps the place where we work is not as important as the people we work with, the cause we work for, and the role we play. Interestingly, Benjamin Franklin noticed this same phenomenon between English settlers and American Indians. There were many cases in which English settlers would voluntarily join the tribes of American Indians. However, there were very few cases where the reverse would happen. Even when settlers were kidnapped by American Indians, they would sometimes refuse to be returned to their settlements when given the opportunity to escape. Franklin theorized that it had to do with their tribal mentality and their strong sense of belonging built into their way of life.[2] There are three important aspects of this connectedness. The first is the tribe, which serves as an organizing principle to gather, govern, and unite the talent, know-how, and expertise of members. The second is tribal spirit, which is the uniting purpose of the tribe as well as the manner and method the tribe adopts to accomplish its goals. The third is the role and responsibility of a tribal member.

A great example of these principles in today's frontier of science is the Event Horizon Telescope Project (EHT). The objective of this international consortium is to capture the first images of a black hole in space. This is a very ambitious and incredibly difficult task. A black hole is an incredibly dense and relatively small astronomical phenomenon that has such strong gravitational effects that not even light can escape from within it. It is only possible to see a black hole by observing the shadow it casts. This visible boundary is called an event horizon. The black hole that is the target of the EHT resides 55 million light years away from the earth at the very heart of the Milky Way Galaxy. To acquire such a small object at such a great distance requires a very large telescope. In fact, to capture such the image, a telescope the size of the entire earth is required! Obviously, constructing such a device is impossible; however, this is where tribalism steps in to play.

The EHT is an international collaboration of computer scientists, physicists, astronomers, mathematicians, and engineers that have created a computational telescope by uniting the technology of eight observatories around the world and integrating the expertise of well-focused research teams or tribes. The expertise and roles of the globally located tribes consist of instrumentation, data processing, data analysis, simulation, and multi-wave science as well as engineering and computer programming. Each telescope within the network works in concert and is coordinated through extremely precise atomic clocks. Through the use of artificial intelligence and other computer algorithms, the images collected throughout the network are reconciled to create an image of the black hole at the center of our universe. In April 2019, the lofty ambitions of the project were realized. The image that was captured provided physical evidence of Einstein's theories of relativity and also gave the world a glimpse of something that was once thought to be forever invisible.[3] It also represented the best aspects of tribal innovation, focused groups working within themselves to practice and expand their science or art. These same groups also work vigorously between themselves to leverage their knowledge and achieve something beyond that which is achievable by any single group. This same connectivity or tribal spirit is observable in many great inventions, from the Wright Brothers flying machine of the early 1900s to today's human genome project. There is "something" that drives members to focus harder, work ambitiously, collaborate freely, lift each other up, and endure hardship. Similar to the task of the EHT project, we must capture an image of this illusive concept so that we can apply it to achieve something more than ordinary, the extraordinary.

Developing a Definitional Lens

Through my own experiences as an academic consultant, researcher, and active participant, I have observed in theory and in practice the tribal nature that underscores an innovative endeavor. Because of the novel nature of these experiences, I began to wonder if there was a structure or framework that might provide a definitional context for this way of approaching complex problems and innovation. The research began by examining the structure and accomplishments of notable tribes throughout history. From that review, early ideas and concepts about structures, roles, and drive that defined tribes such as the Zulu, Cherokee, Viking, and Huaxia began to emerge. Although these structures were described in different names across tribes, their description in context and application were very similar. For example, the role of Shaman for healing and wisdom is an important foundation of knowledge management, knowledge transfer, and storytelling in many ancient tribes. Of course, it is also an important role for maintaining the health and happiness of the tribe. The way this important construct was accomplished and the way it was operationalized in roles and responsibilities can be clearly identified in many tribes throughout history.

I then studied fantastic historical initiatives such as the American Revolution (particularly the Sons of Liberty), the Women's Suffrage Movement, the Civil Rights Movement, the Apollo space program, the Wright Brothers invention of the flying machine, and the French Revolution. Turning to music, I studied iconic rock bands such as the Rolling Stones, Rush, and R.E.M. Again, the objective was to identify key structures that bonded members of the initiative, kept them focused, and allowed them to endure setbacks. To my delight, similar structures were readily identifiable. Moreover, these structures matched the same structures identified in the study of historical tribes. For example, the construct of perseverance was very prominent in initiatives such as the Civil Rights Movement and the Women's Suffrage Movement. In both of these instances, enormous resistance was overcome with very patient and methodical resolve. The very same construct that allowed tribes of old to endure incredible hardship and eventually prosper. Among the iconic bands of rock and roll, there was a very strong theme of sacrifice. A talented musician had to be willing to sacrifice some of the limelight for the band to endure. In some cases, members of these bands claim that one had to be willing to put almost everything behind the interest of the band in order to survive. If this was not possible, then the band's viability might be compromised. It is certainly not the intention of this book to suggest that one sacrifice "all" for a cause or an innovative project. However, these findings do suggest that a laser focus and a willingness to be "all in" with your effort and "all supportive" of others is required to move beyond the ordinary.

The final and most interesting part of the field study was firsthand examination of "Super" projects that are a part of today's most innovative landscape. Super projects have objectives that were once thought to be completely impossible. As mentioned earlier, the Event Horizon Telescope is a worldwide initiative that seeks to photograph a black hole at the center of our solar system. MIT's Broad Institute is pioneering the field of disease prevention through analysis, mapping, and engineering of the human genome. The Lawrence Berkeley Lab is creating innovative technologies and new discoveries at the intersection of computing, physical, and biological sciences. In India, the Mars Orbiter is an astounding testimony of efficiency and advanced engineering.[4] At Cal Tech, the Space Solar Power Project is pioneering the concept of capturing solar power in space and wirelessly transmitting it back to Earth. This initiative is already delivering promising results and could become a limitless source of energy in the future.[5] The Robot Research Initiative in Korea is a pioneering and very productive collaboration between the government and industry giants such as Samsung and Hyundai in the development of advanced robotics. These and other super projects have very identifiable and effective modes, methods, and codes of conduct that predispose them to discovering the best ideas and the most innovative means to achieve them. Perhaps the most noticeable of these constructs is ambition and scientific navigation. Each of these initiatives is incredibly ambitious. These groups are seeking to accomplish objectives that were once thought impossible. However, their quest or dream is not guided by hope, hearsay, or wishful thinking. It is guided by strict adherence to facts, data, and collective knowledge. This is consistent with fantastic initiatives in history, most notably the Wright Brothers invention of the flying machine, as well as the scientific approach to agriculture applied by the Cherokee and Navajo. Again, examining these super projects provided a basis for uncovering common themes or dimensions that defined innovative work and idea generation.

In the next phase of the research, I conducted extensive, structured interviews with teams of technologists, scientists, and managers working in the information, chemical, materials, and medical sciences. Although these initiatives were not super projects, they were very ambitious endeavors that were "breakthrough" and considered very successful. The groups of the study were tasked with developing new products and services in evolving fields such as biotechnology, machine learning, robotics, and additive manufacturing. The results of their work were more than impressive. Each of these teams had produced cutting-edge products and overcome serious obstacles on the way to their innovations. Through this process of observation, participation, and interview, I further developed the initial conceptualization of "tribes" and "tribal instincts" which will be discussed in the next section. The major objective was to develop constructs and descriptions that were valid as well as generalizable to many contexts of innovative work. Importantly, it was very clear after this phase of the study that the same structure of tribalism or as I termed it "tribal instincts" that are found in historical contexts as well as super projects are identifiable, recognizable and are at work in today's most innovative initiatives!

Following the field studies, two surveys of project leaders, scientists, technologists, and technology managers were conducted. To qualify as a respondent, the technologists, business developers, and managers of the targeted firms had to have at least 10 years of industry experience. The non-random survey is U.S. based although most of the firms represented had international interests and operations. The businesses represented in the survey spanned a wide range of technological endeavors and ranged from start-ups of two years to firms with business legacies of 50 plus years. In all instances, care was taken to include respondents and associated business that were entrepreneurial and operating in evolving technology-based industries. Over 300 respondents participated in both surveys. In survey one, a list of items that included measures of "tribal instincts" was sent for consideration. The respondents were asked to evaluate the "impact" of these behaviors in identification and development of breakthrough ideas. The respondents were also given the opportunity to add and assess the impact of any other behaviors or activities that might have been overlooked. In a confirmatory context, the results of this survey were then factor analyzed to assess the structure of the underlying instincts and their impact on team performance. Through this technique, the seven tribal instincts were formally verified. These instincts were then described more fully and sent back to respondents in a second survey to assess their validity and their impact. The results of the second survey implied very strong support for the tribal instincts and for their impact. As a follow-up, random respondents were chosen for Skype interviews and field visits to further assess the validity of the instincts and gather more context about their impacts. The results of these analyses were very clear. There is a structure that captures the "something" associated with endeavors that are extraordinary. It is identifiable and describable, and it provides a useful framework for understanding the predisposition of a group or group of groups to accomplish something innovative.[6] That "something" is "tribal instincts". When these instincts are in full force, the organization is tribal and a powerful "tribal spirit" will guide the effort. Let's take a closer look at these important instincts.

Tribal Instincts

As illustrated in Figure 1.1, seven key attributes or constructs characterize the *esprit de corps* or *tribal spirit* that is readily observable in extraordinary initiatives. I call this set of constructs *tribal instincts* because they are a fixed pattern of behavior that is intuitive and responsive to the task at hand. These instincts are: (1) *Ambition*—Thinking bigger, asking bigger questions, (2) *Structure*—Emergent rules and processes grounded in shared beliefs and values that govern and organize the tribe, (3) *Roles and Responsibilities*—Well-defined roles and

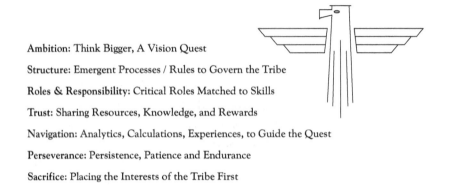

Ambition: Think Bigger, A Vision Quest

Structure: Emergent Processes / Rules to Govern the Tribe

Roles & Responsibility: Critical Roles Matched to Skills

Trust: Sharing Resources, Knowledge, and Rewards

Navigation: Analytics, Calculations, Experiences, to Guide the Quest

Perseverance: Persistence, Patience and Endurance

Sacrifice: Placing the Interests of the Tribe First

Figure 1.1: Seven Tribal Instincts

expectations based on the talents and experiences of members, (4) *Trust*—A strong code of sharing resources, knowledge, and rewards, (5) *Navigation*—Charting a path through extensive use of analytics, calculations, and experience, (6) *Perseverance*—Persistence, patience, and endurance in the face of calamity, and (7) *Sacrifice*—A sense of selflessness, putting the interests of the tribe ahead of sub-groups or individuals. In subsequent chapters, I will fully develop the definition and application of each instinct . For now, it is important to view the instincts as a framework for determining the predisposition of a group to discover an extraordinary idea and/or accomplish an extraordinary journey. It explains the success as well as the shortcomings of everything from a sports team to a political campaign.

It is useful to think of the instincts as seven glasses of water. If all of the glasses are full, then the effort is fully tribal, and the likelihood of an extraordinary outcome is extremely high. If some of the glasses are half-full, partially full, or empty, then the effort does not have tribal spirit and the likelihood of something very innovative occurring is much lower. You might achieve an end, but it will not be particularly innovative or, as a strategist would say, a strategic strike. In fact, it is very eye-opening to measure initiatives that were less than successful against the instincts. It becomes easy to see that the lack of performance is because some of the glasses (instincts) were less than full or empty. For example, the fall of the telecommunications giant Nortel Networks has its roots in a lack of navigation, ambition, trust, and sacrifice. As data and voice moved into mobile formats and across digital networks, the company remained steadfast in its traditional telephone business. Yet, all signals pointed to a new and different competitive landscape. Cisco and other companies embraced this new frontier with ambitious new products and services. They also believed and quickly acted on the new signals from the marketplace. A popular narrative is that Nortel was caught completely unaware of the changes around them. However, this is far from the truth. There were pockets of business people, technologists, and engineers within the company that knew the frontier was changing and tried to relay the knowledge to senior management.[7] However, a lack of trust and many obstacles in the sharing of knowledge and information resulted in an "echo chamber" that doomed the company. To meet the new competitive challenge, Nortel would have to sacrifice old products and old ideas to make room for the new. They simply could not climb that mountain. Interestingly, Nortel built its empire on being very tribal but quickly disintegrated when the instincts were no longer present. In contrast, the most innovative projects and businesses tend to have full glasses across the instincts. This is how innovative products, services, and businesses as well as the impossible come to life.

Tribe or Rogue Actors?

Now comes the caveat of a notion such as tribalism. An unfortunate consequence of today's world of blended news, entertainment, opinion, and sensationalism is the casting of tribes and tribalism for something unwanted or inherently evil. In addition, there is a cottage industry of consultants that point to tribes within an organization as a fundamental problem. This is quite ironic given the fact that synergistic groups provide a fundamental organizing principle as well as a means of focus and efficiency within almost any society or organization. Yet, it is very tempting to isolate a group of non-functioning and uncooperative members (e.g., The Unites States Congress, hate groups, a street gang) and say that their problem is tribalism. The group will not cooperate, they pursue their own interests, they have a narrow agenda, and they don't know what they don't know. They band together tightly and are a burden to other groups. We would be better off without them!

Ironically, if we measure such groups against the tribal instincts, we can see that they are not tribal at all, far from it. In fact, their problem is that they are not tribal enough. Such groups are mobs or rogue actors. It is possible that such groups exhibit some small aspect of the tribal instincts such as emergent structure and roles/responsibilities but they are typically not willing to sacrifice for the overall good of other groups, their ambition is twisted, they ignore important signals that tell them they are rogue, and trust is very illusive because such groups tend to attract members that trust no one. There is a world of difference between the exploits of rogue actors such as street gangs and the accomplishments of tribes such as the Cherokee, Viking, or Inuit. There is also a world of difference between rogue initiatives based on obstruction, hate, and self-interest versus the magic of tribal initiatives such as the Event Horizon Telescope. The appropriation of tribalism for what is really rogue behavior is simply wrong. The path to innovative and effective organizations is to keep and foster tribalism within and across groups while driving out or rehabilitating rogue actors. This does not mean there will always be complete harmony among tribal members or between tribes. That is not always the goal or even a desired state. It does mean that through times of discontent the vision will remain on achieving greater good and accomplishing something collectively that cannot be accomplished individually. The seven instincts provide a framework for assessing how "tribal" groups are within any organization and the innovative predisposition of an organization (the "tribe of tribes" or nation) to accomplish something more than ordinary. It is also a useful perspective to view the partnerships or collaborative agreements of the organization with its network of suppliers and customers. Perhaps some aspect of the organizational network has turned rogue. This can begin to poison even the most well-functioning tribe or nation.

A Tribe of One

At this point, you might be asking, "How does this apply to me?" By its very definition, Tribe implies a social dynamic between people and between groups of people. However, there is something a bit more to the tribalism observed in my research and described in this book. It is also a "way of thinking" that drives individual behavior and creates an ability to work seamlessly within groups, across groups, and by yourself. I call this "tribal thinking", and it is an important part of esprit de corps and something that each of us can apply to ourselves. This type of thinking integrates the tribal instincts with three key aspects problem solving: vision, engagement, and approach. It is a way of taking the instincts that are found in innovative organizations and integrating them into the way we approach challenges when we are a tribe of one. This perspective is illustrated in Figure 1.2.

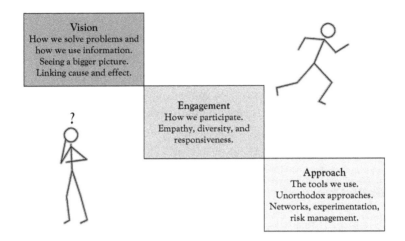

Figure 1.2: Tribal Thinking

Vision

Maybe one of the most talked about concepts of leadership is "critical think-ing". It is a term that sounds important and, as it turns out, is really import-ant, but it is also a term that is defined differently across contexts. From the observations of this research as well as my own experiences, I define critical thinking as the ability to correctly and consistently identify cause and effect relationships. It is also a part of a larger intuitive process called "vision". Vision is seeing a bigger picture and a bigger context in the challenges we face. I will provide a very simple and personal story to illustrate this point.

My neighborhood is built on land that was once farmland. The land rolls with swales and small hills and has at its center an old farm pond. As homes were built, roads constructed, and trees removed, the pond began to stagnate with algae and other plant life taking over the water. To my surprise, the neigh-borhood board decided to "treat" the water with chemicals. A presentation by a local chemical company guaranteed that the problem would be solved. After a few treatments, the solution seemed to work. However, after another year, the problem was back. The board convened and met with the vendor, and it was decided that more chemicals were needed. I think you can see where this is going. The additional treatments did no better and other problems started to arise. After many treatments, a change of board membership, and the help-ful advice of an ecologist, it was eventually recognized that every pond needs a source of water, typically a stream. A pond also needs a sink, typically another stream or pond. In other words, a pond is part of a living ecosystem. The building of houses and roads had taken away both the sink and the source. When this was reestablished with French drains and other natural structures, the pond became healthy again, no chemicals needed. Seeing the pond as something more than an isolated body of water is envisioning the issue within its proper context. We can then correctly identify cause and effect relationships and apply the right solution. It is something that the tribal instincts reinforce whether we are working in a team or working alone.

Engagement

One of the most interesting aspects of leadership and everyday life is how we engage with others when there is a challenge ahead. In today's society there is a strong tendency to "look after number one" and to evaluate everything from the standpoint of how it impacts "me". This is actually a very natural tendency that is based on our instinct for survival. Plus, it certainly does no harm to have fun and celebrate the unique things that make you the person you are. However, before we snap another selfie or walk past another piece of garbage on the ground that can easily be put in a receptacle, it is important to remember that all of us live in a highly connected and interdependent society; be it at work or at play. This is where a tribal mindset can assist. It may not be our responsibility in the form of a job to pick up a piece of trash that is blowing across the park, but it is our responsibility as a member of society to pick it up. In doing so, we help the tribe. Further it is something we would expect others in the tribe to do for us. Tribes have strong themes of selflessness and service. This is something that can be easily forgotten, yet, it is something we can and should apply to our own walk of life.

Tribes also have well-defined roles for its members based on their talents, capabilities, and accomplishments. When a tribal member's role and responsibility is matched with his or her talents, the member and tribe benefit. However, when this is not true, a feeling of displacement and discouragement is likely to follow. While this seems logical and obvious, it is actually quite at odds with recent trends in parenting and schooling. Participation trophies and promises that you can be anything that you desire have clouded our perception of where talents lie and how they can be used. We should encourage everyone, but we should do so in a way that recognizes their natural and acquired talents. To recognize talent that might exist or could exist when all evidence says it does not exist is to deceive. Everyone has a talent and insight to contribute; it is very tribal to match that talent with a role that is needed for the challenge that is faced. This phenomenon is readily apparent in super projects, social movements, and great inventions such as the flying machine. Unique talents that are leveraged and focused can create something that is magical. Tribal instincts teach us to discover our best talent, recognize the unique talents of others, and engage in a way that leverages and celebrates all talents.

Approach

In the chapters to come, I will illustrate and discuss methods, tools, and techniques that very innovative organizations use to meet challenges. To me, this is one of the most unique and interesting features of this form of innovation. The key to success in methods and approach is the art of creative improvisation. This is at odds with well-known frameworks in business that teach us to frame entire industries and disruptions with standard frameworks. It is also at odds with our natural tendency to use the same tools to fix every problem.

We live in a world of routine. A key unlocks a door, then we enter the house, office, or building. The bus or train stops a certain number of times between a primary point of departure and a destination, every day. Red means "stop", green means "go", and traffic conforms to government-designated lanes and speed limits. All of this is useful, and all of this is good. However, this world of routine can sometimes rub itself on us a bit too much when we approach a challenge. We look for the technique or approach that worked last time. We use the method of the company that leads the industry. We turn to the consultants to tell us about the current state of the art. We look to *Harvard Business Review* or a life coach for answers. Again, none of this is necessarily wrong, unless the challenge you face is unique and novel. At that point, it is likely that a method or technique that is unorthodox or "invented" might be necessary. Further, experimentation might be required, and some method of taking a risk without being carelessly risky might be the difference between success and failure. Tribal instincts teach us to improvise when the challenge we face is bigger, unique, or more complex than the capacity of capability of conventional methods. A great example of this is Continental Army victory over the British Army in the American Revolutionary War. Instead of meeting the British on their terms, George Washington chose to use tactics and techniques he learned from native American Indians during the French and Indian wars. He relied heavily on the art of surprise, carefully chosen engagements, and ambush tactics that he had used during his earlier military engagements with the French.[8] Napoleon also revolutionized warfare by emphasizing movement of his army. By taking his troops back and forth across a theater of war, he was able to destroy enemy forces one by one rather than allowing them to combine.[9] Again, tribal thinking tells us that how we approach a challenge in terms of method or technique is critically important. Routine and a mischaracterization of the challenge are threats that can derail any of us whether we are the leader of a corporation, a minister, or just someone walking through everyday life. Sometimes the unorthodox approach or the approach we invent is the key to discovering something more than ordinary. Improvisation is an art form and a way of thinking that can be critical in finding the method or approach that leads to success.

Together, envisioning a challenge, engaging with others, and approach provide a blueprint for how you and I, as a tribe of one, confront challenges. This is similar to classical models of decision making such as Simon's model of Intelligence, Design, and Choice.[10] However, a key difference is the dynamic that occurs when individual problem-solving combines with the collective efforts of the tribe. This is captured in the engagement stage. Ideally, we want everyone in the group to be thinking tribally and we want them all to leverage to the fullest their unique talents. We also want to make sure that the required talents for success are represented. That is no small task! However, when this occurs, the best of rational decision making among individuals transfers to the efforts of the Tribe. Tribal thinking is a useful framework for applying the instincts to our own walk through leadership or life. In the coming chapters, each of these instincts will be developed further. I will also introduce tools and techniques that are used in innovative organizations to find ideas, establish chains of cause/effect, manage risk, and develop strategies that address the real problem that is faced. Most of these techniques are unorthodox and improvised. However, they demonstrate the importance of tribal instincts and the power of tribal spirit that can be unlocked when those instincts are in full force.

Notes

1. Sydney Finkelstein, "Why Companies Should Hire Teams Rather than Individuals," *Wall Street Journal*, October 29, 2017.
2. S. Junger, *Tribe: On Homecoming and Belonging*. Hachette Book Group, Inc, 2016.

3. Seth Fletcher, *Einstein's Shadow: A Black Hole, a Band of Astronomers, and the Quest to see the Unseeable*. HarperCollins, 2018.
4. "Why India's Mars Mission Is So Cheap—and Thrilling," *BBC News*, September 24, 2014.
5. "Solar Power Stations in Space Could Supply the World with Limitless Energy," *Forbes*, March 12, 2018.
6. A. H. Segars, "Creating a Tribal Approach for Innovation in Organizations," *Business Horizons*, 62(3), 2019.
7. "Nortel Ex-Worker Says He Told Company of Revenue Problems," *Wall Street Journal*, May 6, 2019.
8. Thomas Fleming, *The Strategy of Victory: How George Washington Won the American Revolution*. Da Capo Press, 2017.
9. David Chandler, *The Campaigns of Napoleon*. Simon and Schuster, 1966.
10. L. Buchanan and A. O'Connell, "A Brief History of Decision Making," *Harvard Business Review*, January 2006.

· 2 ·

AMBITION

Win together today and we walk together forever
— Fred Shero, Coach of the Philadelphia Flyers,
1974 Stanley Cup Playoffs

The tribal instinct of ambition is based on framing problems and challenges in terms bigger than their initial description or conception. It is very easy to frame problems in "small" terms. After all, it is a basic human tendency to structure uncertainty or challenges in a way that results in a rational, quick, and attainable solution. Given this tendency, a vicious cycle of "thinking small" can easily prevail as leaders frame problems narrowly and those charged with finding solutions continue to narrow the problem even further. Each party will continue this cycle until an answer is found; then, all parties will call it a "problem solved" and another example of innovation. Tribal ambition asks bigger questions, searches outside of conventional boundaries for solutions, and utilizes stories to build a shared context for possibilities that push the boundary of imagination. It is something that is identifiable in leaders as well as followers. It can be embodied in a worthy cause. It can also give meaning and purpose to tedious tasks and bumps that are encountered along the road.

Wear It on Your Sleeve

As noted by many scientists and project leaders interviewed, Ambition is something that is "worn on the sleeve". As humans, we can sense ambition and ambitious people are drawn to efforts that are challenging and meaningful. In contrast, a lack of ambition will most often result in a lack of effort or a sense that "the fix is in". Nothing discourages innovation more than an effort that is led by someone with small or no ambition; the immediate connotation is that the effort is not important or may go away. The American Civil Rights Movement is a great example of ambition "worn on the sleeve". Although equal rights for all citizens seems like an obvious and desired part of today's society, it was a very radical idea in the United States when this movement gained initial traction in the mid-1950s. Rather than seek selected rights for African-Americans such as housing, bus transportation, or wages, the movement sought to secure the same rights for its people that were already given freely to Whites. Taking this ambitious mantle, Dr. Martin Luther King, along with Ralph Abernathy, Fred Shuttlesworth, Joseph Lowery, and many other activists, formed the Southern Christian Leadership Conference (SCLC). Leveraging the legal victories of the NAACP, this innovative organization offered training and leadership assistance for local groups seeking to fight segregation. Most importantly, the group made organized, nonviolent protests its central method for confronting racism. King collaborated with friends and rivals, spoke up, and pursued something that, in its time, was deemed impossible. King was a master of connecting people, ideas, and opportunity that eluded other leaders. He was also one of history's best in terms of creating passion for and articulating an ambitious dream. It is important to remember the impression we first present and the one we leave with those we interact with every day. To create zeal for an initiative, it is important to wear ambition on the sleeve.

Create a Worthy Cause

In today's world, super projects have at their core goals and objectives that seem like magic. Exploring the center of our galaxy, engineering the DNA that is our basic building block, building robots that further extend our capabilities, and pioneering new forms of renewable energy are causes that push us past our current boundaries. Visionaries such as the late Steve Jobs are known for their ability to focus on the most important initiatives and create a sense of urgency and excitement about their impact on the world. So, does this mean that we have to create this level of excitement and expectation about projects that may not be as revolutionary? The answer is Yes and No. As we will see in a later chapter, it is possible for an organization to invest in a big and risky project that has little return. It is very hard to build a theme of ambition around something that most know will not add much value. In contrast, it is also possible that an organization can take on a project that is small, less risky, and yet have substantial return. Therefore, the first step is to clearly frame where the value of the project lies. If there is no value relative to the effort required, particularly in large, risky projects, then some serious rethinking of the initiative should be undertaken. It is incredibly difficult to make a case for ambition in these instances. If there is underlying value but it is difficult to shape into a message, then it is likely the result of framing the value in terms smaller than it deserves. Dr. King could have focused only on improving the wages of African-Americans. Instead, he saw the issue as one of equal rights for all. Therefore, it is critical to build a case for value that is more ambitious than how the challenge is initially presented. In other words, any challenge or project definition is likely to be initially presented in smaller and simpler terms than the problem that needs to be solved. Not every project needs to change the world, but if there is some clear sense of purpose or improvement that seems logical and necessary and requires the skills of those involved, then the glass of ambition will be closer to full.

Make the Tedious Worthwhile

Even in the super projects that were researched for this book, it is possible to dive into the inner workings and find portions of the work that are not glamourous. Instead, they are tedious and can easily be disconnected from the great ambition of the overall project. This can happen in almost any organization and in any endeavor. It was very noticeable that leaders and members of the more glamourous parts of super projects consistently reinforced the importance and contribution of everyone. They also kept everyone focused on the bigger ambition of the effort and the sense of accomplishment that awaited them upon the completion of the journey. So, if the task at hand is implementation of software or rethinking a training program, it is important to tailor the ambition accordingly (you might not change the world) yet instill some sense of the bigger issue being addressed and the importance of efforts in reaching the goal. A "sense of pride" is essential for innovation, and that "sense of pride" has its foundation in a purpose, a logical road ahead, and a significant role to play in success.

Chase Breakthrough Ideas (That Do Not Want to Be Found)

There is a myth about innovation that makes it attractive and wonderful. The myth is that breakthrough ideas are easy to capture. Yet, nothing seems further from the truth. The really novel ideas are elusive, tricky, easily hidden, threatening, and absolutely difficult to capture. If this notion was stated at the beginning of a leader's speech about innovation, many organizational members would not take on the task. In fact, many might run the other way, quickly. However, this is the uncomfortable truth. Breakthrough ideas must be hunted, and they must be earned. To take on this task and to relish the hunt is to be tribal.

A second myth about chasing ideas is that process is the enemy. To be structured, deliberate, and bounded by technique is to lose creativity and flow. Instead of those grounded in a process mindset, we need free thinkers, artsy types, and lots of thinking space. Images of commune types of corporate campuses, sleep pods, and working remotely come to mind. This is a great storyline, and it certainly seems to draw distinction between the old school ways of accomplishing tasks and the new way. In addition, some of this story does ring true. There is always a need for diversity in talent and background which we will see in a later chapter. However, innovation is a bit more complicated than its popular storyline. In truth, the hunt for breakthrough ideas requires the discipline and efficiencies of a process. Plus, those who are grounded in process and structured thinking are as likely as the ultra-creative to see a breakthrough solution. In fact, who is to say that the ultra-creative eschew process? In my experiences, I have seen quite the opposite! Wherever a group falls on discipline continuum, you must have the right process for the task at hand. Such a process helps us discover the "right" question to ask and then asks us to consider multiple possibilities in terms of solution. This type of myth-breaking approach is a hallmark of innovative efforts in history and in the super projects of today's world.

Explore the Possibilities

An unfortunate artifact of most formal educational experiences is the quick hunt for "the" answer. In our math classes, we are given equations and the task is to find the answer. We hunt for the answer in multiple choice questions, true/false, and short answer. There is nothing wrong with this approach until we enter the world of complexity and uncertainty. In this context, answers may be elusive, information may be incomplete, and there is no clear recipe. Unfortunately, when this occurs, there is a strong tendency to reframe the challenge so that it looks like a structured problem. Psychologists call this "convergent thinking". The basic idea is that we strongly favor gathering familiar information, relying heavily on past successes, framing a small problem, and then falling on a solution fast. An everyday example is purchasing a new vehicle. If you have driven a certain make and model for a long time, you will tend to stick with that vehicle, even if your situation in terms of transportation needs has radically changed. In today's world of social media, influencers, political journalism, and expert panels, it is easy to fall into a trap of convergent thinking on almost any issue. Perhaps the most dangerous aspect of convergent thinking is that it works just often enough for us. Therefore, it becomes the first thing we lean on when uncertainty strikes.

An alternative and more tribal way of facing a challenge is to ask the simple question "What is Possible?" Doing so moves us to a broader frontier of possible solutions and pauses our inborn desire to fall on a solution fast. This was a very noticeable trait among members of super projects. It is also something that resounds throughout history. Let's look at a super project first. Photographing the black hole at the center of our galaxy is an impossible task for any single observatory on Earth. No single facility has the equipment that is needed for such a feat. A convergent approach might be to simply build a bigger and more powerful telescope. This might be particularly true if you are the chief scientist at one of these observatories and you have always wanted to expand your facility. In contrast, the approach used by the Event Horizon Telescope Project is to combine the capabilities of several telescopes and, using sophisticated computer technology, make them operate as one. This is a novel approach that is born out of thinking more broadly. Psychologists call this *Divergent Thinking*. This type of approach considers and evaluates possibilities before falling on a solution. Importantly, these possibilities are purposefully drawn from very different perspectives than normally considered. At first, these possibilities may seem more like fantasy than a real solution.

However, upon further investigation, many of these possibilities are not only feasible; they are well-hidden breakthrough ideas. History is full of the accomplishments of divergent thinkers. The Wright Brothers design of the flying machine was radically different from other designers of the day. The leading expert of aeronautics at the time, Octave Chanute, told the brothers their machine would not fly. In another example, many lives were saved when Chesley Sullenberger and Jeffrey Skiles landed a damaged passenger jet safely on the Hudson River. Their solution was so unorthodox that the pilots were initially investigated for wrongdoing but eventually heralded for heroism by the Federal Aviation Administration. These as well as many other great feats in history were all the result of asking the simple question, "What is Possible?"

Narrative Building

How can we take something like ambition and operationalize it into an approach that is structured, revealing, and yet fun. Yes, fun, as we will discuss in the next chapter, part of building connectedness is storytelling, fun, and creative conversation. The technique that brings these things together and helps capture that elusive breakthrough idea is narrative building, it is illustrated in Figure 2.1. The purpose of the technique is to frame a frontier of

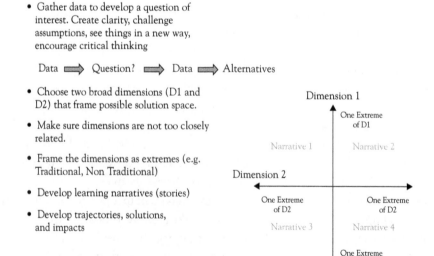

Figure 2.1: Thinking Bigger: Narrative Building

possibilities, build a creative context for describing the frontiers, and set the stage for objectively assessing a course of action.

Ask a Bigger Question

The first stage of narrative building is to develop a question of interest. An easy way to kill innovation is to fall on a question too quickly or localize it to our favored or most comfortable context. Few decision makers realize that it takes gathering data and information to arrive at the right question. Plus, that "right" question is almost always a bigger question than the one we fist ask. A bigger question of interest will frame the issue in clear and challenging terms. It will challenge assumptions, frame things in a different way, and be something that might apply to several contexts, businesses, or situations. Too many times we frame questions in very small terms. We tend to focus on the symptoms of a problem rather than step back and see a larger system of relationships or a larger context of cause and effect. Most likely, this is our default setting, and some effort is required to think a bit bigger than the problem as it is presented to us. A great example of this thinking is the thought process of the Wright Brothers. They asked the question *"How do birds fly and how do they sustain flight?"* rather than *"How do you build a flying machine?"* Sustained flight became their question and their quest. Following this thinking, they discovered the three key aspects of fight, roll, yaw, and pitch. Other inventors failed miserably because they asked smaller questions. Their view of flight was that of a glider powered by a sling shot. In contrast, the Wright Flyer demonstrated controlled and sustained flight, and history was made.

Frame the Solution Space

Once a bigger question of interest has been developed, the next step is to frame a frontier of possibility. Again, the key thought is to reveal *"What is possible?"* We do this by choosing two very broad dimensions that frame the solution space. Broad dimensions help us build a bigger fishing net to capture ideas. Again, the tendency will be to frame these dimensions small and localize them to your immediate context; RESIST THIS AT ALL COSTS!!!! If these dimensions are too small, then we will exclude a lot of prior art and a lot of untried possibility. Prior art are solutions that have been attempted and untried possibility are solutions we have not tried before. We want a canvas of everything that has been done and everything that could be done. The most helpful ally in developing these dimensions are small words. The words *Why? How? When? Where? What?* and *Who?* are not big or complex words but they ask big questions. For example, if the question is *How might a company expand its market share?*, the "*Who?*" may be customers. The "*What?*" may be products and/or services. These broad dimensions are the essential elements for any company seeking to expand its market share. Notice how we stay away from localizing the question. The question is "*How might a company gain market share?*" It is not "*How might our company gain market share?*" Next, we take the dimensions and frame them as extremes. Again, we do this to build a bigger fishing net for catching ideas. For this question, it seems useful to anchor each of the dimensions using the labels *traditional* and *non-traditional*. As shown in Figure 2.2, this gives us a robust set of narratives about how market share might be expanded. In the Northwest grid, a firm sells more of its traditional products to traditional customers (market penetration). In the Southwest grid, the firm expands its market by selling traditional products to non-traditional customers (market expansion). In the Northeast grid, the firm expands by selling non-traditional products to traditional customers (cross selling). In the Southeast grid, the firm pioneers completely new markets by selling non-traditional products to non-traditional customers (market creation). With this context, it is now possible to develop stories about how firms in and out of the industry have accomplished success or met failure within each of these narratives.

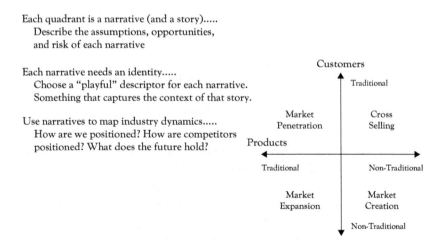

Figure 2.2: Using Narratives to Frame Strategies for Growth

Throughout my research and practical experiences, I have seen several variations of this technique. I have also built upon this approach to incorporate storytelling as well as identification of prior art in solution building. One experience that I remember well was with a very innovative media enterprise. The task before the firm was to create a new series of science fiction movies. The problem was initially stated by senior management in a very rational way: *"How do we create a science fiction series that will meet or exceed the return objectives of our parent organization?"* While certainly a question that seems right out of the MBA classroom, it is inherently small, and it is localized. The initial sample set or "prior art" that will be heavily considered and that will dominate discussion will be science fiction movies that have been successful on those terms. Therefore, the initial and strong tendency will be to write, direct, and distribute a similar series of films. In doing so, a vast collection of films, stories, and approaches that are not classified as successful science fiction will go unnoticed and undiscussed.

True to the instinct of ambition, the small question was elevated to a bigger question when a tribe within the organization took over. Rather than focus the question only on science fiction or even films, the question became *"How do you tell an amazing story?"* This is a much more ambitious question, and now the frontier of prior art is everything from Shakespeare to Broadway plays. Using small words, the tribe framed the main concept of a "story" as *"How?"* and *"What?"*

The *"How?"* was cast as storytelling. This dimension frames a frontier of how a story might be told. On one extreme, storytelling can be traditional. It is one to many, builds on the storyteller's description of main characters, and is primarily a single story. On the other extreme, storytelling may be non-traditional. In this instance, there may be many storytellers, many perspectives of main characters, and several stories rather than one main story. Importantly, as this dimension was developed, many examples of prior art became manifest. Also, the exercise became engaging and fun as prior art was classified in terms of its storytelling. The important point is that a larger canvas of ideas began to take shape around how a story might be told. Again, this is done without localizing it to the company or even the industry.

The "What" dimension is the story that is told or the plot. A traditional plot is like a fairytale with "good characters" that win and "bad characters" that lose. The, flow of the story is very linear. In addition, there is typically a moral in the story and everyone lives happily ever after. A non-traditional plot might have twists and turns where "good" characters lose and "bad" characters win. The story may have no real moral, be non-linear, and may have some surprise that is unexpected and unseen. Again, the ideas started to flow very freely when the dimension of "story" or "plot" was stretched to extremes. It became very easy to identify and discuss literature, plays, television shows, and films that fell at various points along this continuum. When the dimensions are placed together in the form of a grid, then it is very easy to visualize and discuss a frontier of how you might tell an amazing story.

As shown in the Figure 2.3, a final, and very important, part of this exercise is to give "fun" names to each grid. This aids in identifying forms of prior art, builds a common lexicon, and keeps the conversation playful. The names should be indicative of the grids' content, provide a useful context for conversation, yet keep the tenor light and fun. In my own work, I have used songs from Aerosmith, R.E.M., and the Rolling Stones as well as television shows and movies. Basically, any scheme of labeling that is representative of each grid and yet creates a simple and fun mental picture. As illustrated below, for this exercise, the firm chose movies. Traditional storytelling with traditional stories was dubbed *LA LA Land*. This is the feel-good frontier with lovable characters and fairy-tale endings. There is nothing wrong or right with this frontier and it is important to make that clear as the exercise progresses; it just exists. That is what is important for now. Traditional storytelling with a non-traditional story was dubbed *Sixth Sense*. Here, there is a strange twist.

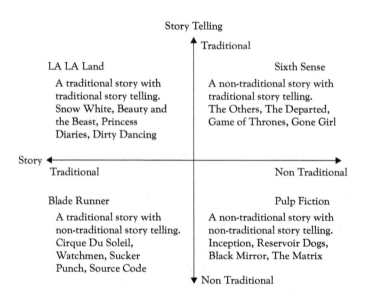

Figure 2.3: Using Narratives to Create Cinema

Something unexpected is revealed in the plot that surprises the viewer yet provides an alternative rationale for the story's chain of events. A traditional story with non-traditional storytelling is *Blade Runner*. In this frontier, much of the story is filled in by the viewer. A great example is Cirqe Du Solei where images, music, and sparse dialogue make room for the viewer's imagination. In turn, the viewer's imagination becomes a key aspect of interpreting events and sequences of the story. *Pulp Fiction* represents non-traditional storytelling and a non-traditional story. True to the film, this space captures more complex stories and more complex modes of storytelling. Again, these movies give a visual and descriptive context to each frontier. Interestingly, the "bread and butter" of this company is the *LA LA Land* frontier and every instinct was pulling them in that direction. In fact, most science fiction movies fall in the *LA LA Land* grid. Notice however, and this is extremely important, the space represents only 25% of available frontier. If a decision maker or decision-making group frames a problem too small or localizes it to their context, then it is likely that a huge amount of prior art and untried possibility will go undiscovered and undiscussed. It is very tribal to think ambitiously. To do so is to ask bigger questions so that a much broader context of solutions is discoverable.

Similar to the Vikings use of the compass for navigation and the irrigation techniques discovered by Navajo Indians, framing questions in a bigger context results in discovery and ideas that are beyond the ordinary. This can be a very difficult task when rivers of organizational process and structure are formed to address small problems and reward small ideas. Interestingly, it may be futile to fight these rivers with traditional organizational thinking; maybe a better tact is to create tribes within the organization that routinely reframe challenges and opportunities in bigger and more impactful terms. In some sense, this is a form of tribal radicalness that functions within the more non-radical frame of the larger organization. The main point of this instinct is to think bigger than the problems and context that typically cloud our vision. If we frame challenges within a localized lens, a smaller set of solutions or art will be visible to us. The very first step in creating an innovative predisposition is to frame challenges so that a vast amount of approaches, experiences, and solutions are available for consideration.

· 3 ·

EMERGENT STRUCTURE

I'm a success today because I had a friend who believed in me
and I didn't have the heart to let him down.

— Abraham Lincoln

As captured in Lincoln's quote, we live in a world of human interconnect-edness. These interconnections are governed by many things, including experiences, expectations, relationships, codes of conduct, values, beliefs, and history. As complex as these interactions can be between one person and another, the complexity skyrockets when applied to groups of people. Most interestingly, these structures are not always formally defined or formally applied with rules and regulations, they emerge over time. In addition, the manifestation of these structures can lead to fantastic outcomes or outright war. The difference in how a group performs can be that drastic! Often, this phenomenon is called "team chemistry". Some measure it by the right combination of work styles, personalities, or skills. In my research and experiences, it seems to be something a little more. It is a set of values, codes of conduct, expectations, and way of working that emerge, are adopted, and form a notice-able and valued "identify" for the group. Again, this is something very indic-ative of tribes of old as well as the super projects of today. I call it *emergent structure*.

Structure and Innovation: A Novel Partnership

It is tempting to think of structure and formal processes as something that might impede discovery. After all, a work environment of "free-wheeling", "be yourself" groups and individuals that defy corporate tradition is a very appealing and entertaining notion. Plus, the logic holds that such "extreme playfulness" results in better ideas, happier employees, and a threat to firms that have been around too long. While a great narrative, the opposite seems true, structure is an important tribal instinct; it is also an essential ingredient in the search for extraordinary ideas. However, it is not structure in the traditional sense (organizational design, processes, decision rights), it is structure that forms organically and is rooted heavily in the values, beliefs, and work ethic of the tribe. These values and beliefs coalesce into a set of unwritten but highly recognizable codes that guide the tribe and are enforced through the peer pressure of its members. As illustrated in Figure 3.1, key aspects of this structure are: *Consensus*, *Human Touch*, *Frugality*, *Ceremony*, *Storytelling*, and *Loyalty*. Together, these emergent structures, as well as the codes of conduct they imply, create a high level of self-determination among tribal members. They feel necessary, they feel competent, and they feel connected. Most of all, there is a structure beyond formal rules that create a sense of novelty, commitment, and identity to the larger group. In a sense, it is team chemistry and

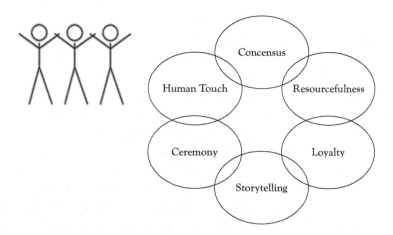

Figure 3.1: Emergent Structure: Unwritten Rules and Codes of Conduct

team culture combined into a code of conduct that is recognizable, expected, and revered.

Consensus

Within a tribal context, authority is something earned and not bestowed. Plus, authority is not command and control, it is coordination, communication, and coaching. Consensus is the driving force of authority in a tribe, and the tribal leader is tasked with creating the means and methods to reach it efficiently and effectively. Perhaps the toughest aspect of this structural characteristic is determining when a consensus emerges and dealing with the potential fallout if all members are not in complete agreement. However, knowing that consensus rather than an executive decision will guide the tribe is a powerful stimulus for robust discussion, expansion of boundaries, and collection of data.

Sometimes, it is necessary to reframe how consensus is measured in order to achieve it. In keeping with the tribal instinct of ambition, we must elevate achieving consensus to something beyond taking a poll or a vote. Consensus is accurately capturing the temperament of the group on an issue of interest, not simply counting the votes of individual members. There are many problems with taking votes. First, we may frame the question incorrectly. Second, we reduce the response to "yay" or "nay". This may simplify the problem. True consensus takes conversation, it takes illustration, and it takes time. Much of this is not written about in management or decision-making literature because it is not glamorous or easy. Let me give you an example in my primary line of work, academics.

In academics, there are levels of achievement that must be reached before a promotion is granted. Academics start as an assistant professor. With the right amount of publications, quality performance in the classroom, and the endorsement of leading academics from other universities, an assistant is promoted to associate professor and given tenure. Later on, with more publications, excellent teaching, and positive endorsement from outside academics, the associate professor may be promoted to a full professor. If the full professor achieves national recognition for his or her research, is a leader in their field, and is recognized by esteemed outside influencers as a leader in the field, then a chaired professorship is granted. All along the way, the hurdle is more rigorous as is the scrutiny by faculty both inside and outside the academic's University.

For many long years, I served as the chairperson of the committee that evaluated and made recommendations for promotion. Part of this process was taking a "vote" among the nine committee members about the merits of submitted cases. By policy, this had to be a vote of "up" or "down". Surprising to me, in some instances, the votes of the committee did not reflect the verbal consensus I heard in deliberations. For example, the discussions about a candidate might be lukewarm, yet, the vote would be 9–0 "up". The only time I saw the votes match consensus was in the extreme cases. A candidate that was discussed as "extraordinary" would be 9–0 "up". A candidate that was discussed as terrible and unworthy was voted 9–0 "down". In cases that were in-between, there was always a unanimous positive vote. This was compounded by the problem that in-between cases were the most populous and the ones that required careful consideration. Clearly, our higher ups, who were counting on our deliberations and recommendations as input for their decisions, were not getting the consensus of these difficult cases.

The problem is that the simple system of voting is not likely to capture the discussion or the "difficult to measure" in-between. Although we were expected to deliver a vote, we were not bound to a system of voting that says one person gets one vote. We needed a system that would represent the conversation but still deliver a vote. My guess, at the time, was that people, even hard-core academics, have a hard time voting "down" even if they believe that is the correct vote. I tested this assumption by bringing two dishes and nine marbles to the next meeting. I told the group that they no longer had to vote "up" or "down". Instead, I wanted them to each think about the right amount of marbles that should go in "up" dish and the right amount that should go in "down" dish. I detached the act of voting "up" or "down" from the individual and assigned it back to the group. To be completely honest, I thought my scheme could go either way. After all, these are academics we are talking about. To my relief, the technique was embraced and is still in use by the promotion and tenure committee. The votes finally began to reflect the conversation; and, most importantly, those making these final decisions had a better source of information. To me, the lesson was clear: you have to make sure the technique from which you measure consensus truly measures consensus. Often, it does not.

In the super projects examined, I saw many instances of "creative consensus". There is copious use of "yellow stickies" to register comments, kudos, or questions about different designs or different alternatives. The beauty of the "stickie" is that it does not represent permanence. You can move your "vote" if other information causes you to rethink your first response. They can be color coded to represent varying forms of expression. You can "vote" multiple stickies. In no instance did I observe the one vote "up" or "down" form of determining consensus. I did observe some isolated instances of formal techniques such as Delphi or the RAND-UCLA Appropriateness Method. However, most of the activity I observed was very similar to my "marble" exercise or the Deep Dive technique of IDEO. The main observation is that the most innovative organizations drive decision making through some form of creative group consensus. This type of consensus making takes time, face-to-face conversation, and a creative approach. Again, this is very reminiscent of ancient tribal structures such as councils, passing the talking stick, and kinship (status based on relationship, experiences, and achievements).

Human Touch

Human touch is also a very key aspect of tribal connectedness. Of course, this is a sensitive and important issue in today's society and boundaries must be respected. That said, it is very noticeable that a handshake, a respectful embrace, a high five, a fist bump, eye contact, or even a nod does wonders to connect members of a tribe. In one of my earliest projects for the Defense Research Projects Agency (DARPA), members of our group developed a "handshake". In fact, this handshake was more of a gesture. Similar to the characters played by Paul Newman and Robert Redford in the movie *The Sting*, we touched the side of our noses with our right index finger to acknowledge each other, acknowledge our tribe, and honor our work together. We did this when we saw each other on or off the job. To this day, when I run into an old colleague from that project, we share the "handshake". It bonds us and helps us to remember a very special time and place. Such gestures are nothing new. Secret societies have had "secret handshakes" for hundreds of years. In the military, a salute is a signal of respect and connectedness. The origin of the salute is to demonstrate recognition, friendliness, and honor for the person you approach. I found the protocol so powerful that I developed "handshakes" with my own children when they were preschoolers. When I returned home from a business trip or from a day at work, it was the first thing we did when we saw each other. Now, it is the first thing we do when one of them returns home from a trip. I am amazed at how meaningful it became to them and me and how it reinforced their place and my place within our own little tribe.

In this same spirit, Texas kindergarten teacher Ashley Taylor assigns a student each day to be the "greeter" for her class. Each child is greeted by name, given a handshake or a hug, and welcomed to the room. As noted by the teacher, this quickly became a favorite ritual of the class and created a connectedness among the students.[1] Throughout the day, the activities of the class require each of the kids to be both speakers and listeners. This requires eye contact, clear speaking, and respect. The simple activity of greeting and being greeted in the morning has improved these skills which improves their interaction with each other and with other kids and adults. Barry White Jr, a fifth-grade teacher in Charlotte, NC has even developed a unique handshake with each of his students. Every morning, he greets them with their unique handshake. Given the tumultuous environment of today's schools, it is easy to see how important human touch can be in making students feel connected, safe, and interactive. If this approach works for children, then why not in the workplace or in other situations?

Interestingly, corporations and other institutions are learning to appreciate the benefits of human touch. Companies such as Google and Apple completely passed on telework. IBM, which had 40% of its employees working remotely, has now pulled thousands of its workers back into the workplace.[2] While telecommuting allowed some companies to save millions on buildings and facilities, it also cost them meaningful and impactful collaboration among its employees. Yes, it is possible to communicate and coordinate with teleconferences, webinars, and similar technologies, but it may not equate to true collaboration. A serious collaborative effort requires well-developed relationships among people. As it turns out, the observation attributed to comedian and filmmaker Woody Allen applies to true collaboration, 80% of success is showing up, in person. Face-to-face interaction is rich in vocal cues, facial expressions, movements, and non-verbal feedback. In fact, through "emotional contagion", we subconsciously match body positions, movements, and breathing rhythms to others when we are engaged in genuine rapport.[3] Informal conversations are also the genesis of the most creative ideas. Without spaces and opportunities to stage these conversations, then we are limited to the frontier that is available through formal meetings, text, webinars, and conference calls. As discovered by many organizations, this frontier is small and not very compelling. This is not to say that many of today's technologies are useless or damaging. It is to say that that they do not fully replace the richness of human touch and they must be carefully supplemented with opportunities and spaces where true collaboration can take place.

For each of us, human touch is a very basic instinct and it is something that is increasingly hard to experience in the workplace or even in everyday life. It is possible to be surrounded by people and still feel alone. Taking meals together, a fist bump, walking the trail around the company pond, tossing a ball to each other, or simply knowing something about the members of your tribe is to bring human touch back into the dynamics of "getting things done". These gestures and forms of person-to-person interaction are readily apparent among members of today's most innovative projects. They are evident in the way workspaces are constructed, in the way conversations occur, and in the way, responsibilities are assumed and quickly shifted if needed. In a sense, human touch echoes the Bill Withers song "*Lean on Me*". It goes, "*lean on me when you're not strong and I'll be your friend, I'll help you carry on, for it won't be long till I'm gonna need, somebody to lean on*". In the super projects I studied, I saw this spirit carefully preserved through photographs of members and the entire tribe prominently displayed on desks, walls, and even mobile devices. As discovered by many organizations, it is easy to drive out human touch. To do so is to drive out needed mechanisms for true collaboration. It also runs against the grain of the human need for interaction, conversation, and basic engagement. We are programmed to expect, respond to, and initiate verbal and non-verbal information. When these channels are shut down, we struggle and only the basic forms of communication and coordination are present. The frontier of collaboration and innovation remains beyond grasp, and our place in the tribe becomes uncertain. New technology will be an important part- ner with human touch in collaboration. However, true idea generation seems more organic and spontaneous than that provided through exclusive use of technology enhanced communication. Very innovative organizations have struck the right balance between high-tech and high-touch. Similar to tribes of old, it is important to know when the time is right for a tribal council. It is also important to make those councils meaningful, engaging, and productive.

Resourcefulness

Another key element of emergent structure is *resourcefulness*. At its most gen- eral level, resourcefulness consists of two important notions: (1) identifying the resources you need, and (2) creatively making the most of the resources you have. In other words, it is important to "*take only what you need*" and "*get the most out of what you take*". Being resourceful brings focus to the task, elim- inates distractions, and integrates the notion of efficiency with innovation.

This is an incredibly important combination in creating a sense of momentum and agility within a highly ambitious effort.[4] Knowing what you need in terms of resource (time, talent, money, materials, and management) to accomplish a task can be thought of as *resource focus*. In some sense, we bring focus to and shape a project through resources. Getting the most of the resources you have is *resource leverage*. Too many times, seemingly innovative efforts turn into ordinary efforts because of the wrong resource focus. Maybe there are too many resources, not enough resources, or the wrong resources. Relatedly, efforts can stall or fail if we do not leverage or apply resources to maximum effect. Maybe we underutilized the money or talent available to us and, as a result, the outcome was less than our hopes. Both of these are important and noticeable traits of tribal resourcefulness. Let's explore these notions just a bit deeper.

Resource focus addresses "how" a project is shaped by budget, workspace, assets, data, metrics, talent, management, and organizational rules. It is the knack for knowing what is needed in terms of resource to accomplish a task. More broadly, it can be thought of as the collective resource response to the challenge at hand. Most often, wayward organizational focus is framed as a lack of resources. Great ideas and innovative paths are made inaccessible by a lack of budget or organizational importance. However, I respectfully suggest that it is more often too much resource that sinks great ideas. This excess includes too many (or the wrong) analytics, cumbersome methods of reporting, too much management, too much organizational publicity, and too many rules. In addition, there may be too much budget, too much technology, and/or too many people. As aptly stated by a pastor I heard one Sunday, "*committees have killed more churches than the devil himself*". Maybe having too much resource is worse than having too little. This suggests that the most likely but least obvious pitfall for an organization that is rich in resources is a tendency to spend its way out of the very best ideas! In all of the super projects I researched, there is a strong sense of "knowing what you need" to accomplish the extraordinary. There is also a strong tendency to be frugal and rational in shaping the resource focus. Excess in terms of PowerPoints, data, personnel, reports, consultants, and other corporate baggage is something that is avoided. In fact, this frugality seems to be a source of pride. Office space is designed for accomplishing work, not for establishing status or brand. Open designs, tables, chairs, and lots of sunlight are shared by all members. There are no signs of conference room tables, tiered classrooms, or extravagant and fixed LCD projection systems. Instead, carts on wheels move equipment from place to place as needed. If projection is needed, a blank wall suffices and the presentation is brought to those interested not vice versa. Most importantly, the money that is typically spent on facilities and offices is saved or invested into talent, travel, or employee development. This concept of "open spaces" as a form of resource focus is not new; however, when it exists within the other aspects of emergent structure such as human touch, consensus, and storytelling, it becomes a powerful driver for achieving more than the ordinary.

Resource focus is perhaps an overlooked characteristic of accomplishing something special. Yet, its influence can be found throughout history and in the modern world. In describing the defeat of the British Army at the hands of the Continental army during the American Revolution, it is often noted by historians that the British had too many ships, too big of an army, and too many generals. Their resource focus was not aligned with the task at hand. The same might also be said for the United States experience in Vietnam. The resource focus of the American military was shaped for large theatres and world wars, not the jungle. In modern business, the rebirth of Apple is often attributed to Steve Jobs refocusing the resources of the company on the projects that mattered most. The lesson for us is that it is important to know exactly what resources you need to bring to the task at hand; no more no less, not everything is important.

Along with resource focus, it is important to leverage the resources we possess. This is particularly true when the resource focus, in terms of amount, is less than we desire. In the most innovative organizations, talents and time are carefully cultivated in the name of leverage. The ability of team members to fill in for others when needed is prized and is paid forward. It is an identifiable part of the emergent structure and creates a sense of comradery and a code of conduct that "the show must go on". In some instances, this may place a hardship on a tribal member, but it is gladly tolerated because help is always on the way. Therefore, it is important to have not only a primary talent but also a set of secondary talents that can be a bridge when a fellow tribal member is unable to perform; it is a very powerful context for innovation.

While it is easy to think about resource leverage in terms of getting the most for the money, repurposing materials, building common computer systems, or sharing office space; the real benefit is leveraging organizational talent, skills, and thinking. True leverage across these dimensions involves combining skills and talents such that they leverage each other and can be recombined for different forms of leverage when needed. Therefore, the goal is not to find a "perfect" or fixed leverage for talent, but it is to find combinations or a portfolio of talent that allows the organization to create needed forms of leverage on demand. A great example of this is found in patterns of human thinking. As described by physicist Leonard Mlodinow, humans think in rational, logical terms when they follow rules. We plot the drive to a destination, calculate how much gas it will take, and determine when we should depart. This line of thinking works well in structured environments. There is nothing wrong with this pattern of thinking; however, I would also argue that it works well when the task is to accomplish the ordinary, not the extraordinary. If it is the overly dominant or the only pattern of thinking within an organization, then we should expect ordinary innovation outcomes. That said, this type of thinking is critical once a new idea is identified. There must be order and process to get work done. Along with logical thinking, there is elastic thinking. This is the type of thinking we do when we figure out what rules should exist or bend existing rules. It is the thinking that happens when old rules no longer seem valid or simply don't work.[5] I would argue that this is the type of thinking that is required to find breakthrough ideas. If it is present enough within the organization, then extraordinary things are more likely.

Both of these archetypes were on display during the flight of Apollo 13. This third mission to the moon in 1970 was considered to be somewhat "routine". However, two days into the mission, an oxygen tank on the spacecraft exploded, severely crippling critical systems. Loss of power, loss of cabin heat, loss of potable water, and, most importantly, loss of oxygen placed the three astronauts in a very grave situation. There was a very real possibility of marooning men in space. Very quickly, logical and rule-based thought gave way to more elastic thinking. Importantly, it is useful to think of this as a shift in dominance rather than one pattern of thinking replacing another. Many rules, policies, roles, and standard operating procedures that had guided past Apollo missions were no longer useful. The task was not to land the astronauts on the moon, it was to rescue them from space. New structures were quickly adopted, old structures modified, and useful old structures were kept to match the new task. Through incredible ingenuity and resourcefulness, parts of the space craft were repurposed to extend power and breathable air. New tests and resulting analytics were developed on the spot to test possibilities and arrive at solutions. A new course was plotted, and the moon's gravity was used to propel the craft back to the earth.[6] Similar to the mission control of Apollo 13, being resourceful is the ability to adopt the right balance of thinking such that rules can be invented, followed, bent, and broken when necessary. This is counterbalanced by the rational process of encoding and institutionalizing the new rules along with the old rules that remain. If this kaleidoscope of thinking, talent, and skills turns so that it meets new challenges, then the high watermark of resource leverage is achieved.

As made famous by the Beatles (a group that had and then lost its tribal spirit), "we get by with a little help from our friends". Knowing when to call on a friend is a very identifiable part of resource focus and resource leverage. There is power in leveraging the resources of friends or allies, but there is also an innate pull to go it alone. Somehow, reaching for help is a sign of weakness or a sign of uncertainty. Collaboration was a major way of "doing" very innovative tasks among tribes of old. Tribal nations were based on shared interest and the synergies made possible through cooperative efforts. In 1876, the Arapaho, Cheyenne, and Lakota tribes engineered one of the most stunning military victories of all time on U.S. soil. Using their knowledge of the land and their formidable skills as buffalo hunters, the warriors Sitting Bull and Crazy Horse led as many as 3,000 Native American Indians against General George Armstrong Custer. Within an hour, Custer and all of his soldiers were dead. Although Custer was told that he faced a large number of warriors, he wanted to believe that his force was adequate for the task. Some historians believe that Custer was more concerned about the warriors escaping rather than defeating them. Although not the same context, it is easy to see cooperative resourcefulness in today's most innovative projects. The Event Horizon Telescope is a testament to cooperation of various tribes within the project and cooperation across observatories and their various tribes. It is the only way to build a telescope the size of the planet Earth, the very thing that is required to view into the center of our galaxy. The Korean government along with business partners and Chonnam National University are pioneering the field of microrobotics using collaborative arrangements in research and development that bridge the boundaries of business, academics, and government. The research center OpenAI is a collaborative effort of Silicon Valley investors and technology companies to promote and develop artificial intelligence so that it benefits humanity.[7] Certainly, there is an ample ambition in the cause of OpenAI. In addition, there is a deep sense that resourcefulness in the form of collaboration will be critical in achieving the aim. The outputs of the effort are impressive. The institute has produced bots that can defeat humans in video games as well as language processing software that can create fluid text from the prompt of a few sentences, phrases, or key words. Throughout history and in today's world, effective collaboration within and between organizations is a hallmark of resource focus, resource leverage, and resourcefulness.

Ceremony

Ceremony and rituals mark important events and key moments in life. Weddings, birthdays, funerals, national holidays, and graduations are some very prominent forms of celebration and ceremony. Rituals are also a form of ceremony but they can also be something a little more personal such as kissing a baseball bat before heading to the plate or taking a deep breath before you speak in public. Together, ceremony and rituals provide a unique sense of identity and shared meaning within a tribe. Throughout history, aboriginal tribes celebrated the new year, the harvest, and victories over enemies, as well as death (celebrated as new life). They also practiced healing rituals that brought tribal members into harmony with themselves, the tribe, and the environment. Ceremony and ritual were so powerful within the Native American Tribes that it was banned by the United States government in the late 1800s as a means of subjugation. At that time, U.S. Interior Secretary Henry M. Teller ordered an end to all *"heathenish dances and ceremonies"* on reservations due to their *"great hindrance to civilization"*. The impetus for this action was the practice of the "Ghost Dance". This dance was a spiritual movement that came about because conditions were so bad on Indian reservations that they needed something to give them hope. It prophesied a peaceful end to white American expansion and preached goals of clean living, an honest life, and cross-cultural cooperation by Native Americans. The attempts to suppress the traditions of Native Americans eventually led to the Massacre at Wounded Knee on December 29, 1890, when the Seventh U.S. Calvary, was sent into the Lakota Sioux's Pine Ridge and Rosebud Reservations to stop the dance and arrest the participants; approximately 150 Native American men, women, and children were killed. Such a tragic event highlights the power of ceremony and the lengths tribes will take to protect it. So, what is it about ceremony that makes it so important? As illustrated in Figure 3.2, there are seven elements that underlie its power: *priority, memory, purpose, gateway, externality, confidence,* and *gratitude.*

Ceremony provides a visible exhibit of what is important within an organization. Awards that recognize adherence or reflection of an organization's core values tell everyone what is valued and what is rewarded. In my institution, The University of North Carolina at Chapel Hill, these values include excellence, teamwork, integrity, leadership, and community. Scholarships, awards, and other events are built around these values to empathize their priority above all else. Ancient tribes celebrated agriculture and the environment

Priority – Emphasize What is Important

Memory – Frame Past and Present Achievements

Purpose – Know Who We Are, What We Stand For

Gateway – Passage From One Place to Another

Externality – Invite the Outside In

Confidence – Zeal to Take on Challenges

Gratitude – Thankfulness and Humility

Figure 3.2: Elements of Ceremony

as a means of acknowledging their importance for survival. Ceremony also provides a scrapbook of memories. Achievements of the past and those who achieved them can be remembered as new heroes are enshrined. Hall of Fame ceremonies in professional sports are great examples of this ceremonial construct. These ceremonies honor the history of the game by remembering past hall of famers, great moments, and the new class of inductees. The past, present, and future are captured in a single ceremony. Purpose and gratitude are also on display in such a ceremony. Through awards, thanks, recognition, and recollection, members gain a greater understanding of why the organization is important, its role models, and how it all contributes to a greater purpose. This is particularly true if the organization, individual, or group is recognized by outside organizations. Together, knowing what is important, celebrating how it was achieved, showing gratitude, and underscoring purpose is a huge catalyst for understanding the values, vision, and contribution of an organization.[8]

Another very important aspect of ceremony is its role as a *gateway* from one stage to another. Graduation ceremonies represent an important achievement of an individual; but, as importantly, they also signal the beginning of a new stage of life. Most often, we attach ceremonial passage with something positive. The promotion, the playoff win, entering a new market, earning a degree are all great examples. For sure, all of these passages are important. However, ceremonies can also be powerful in marking difficulties and setbacks, as well as an urgent need to move on. To mark the passing of Apple's OS 9 operating system, Steve Jobs presided over a mock funeral for the technology. A coffin appeared on stage and Bach's Toccata and Fugue in D Minor echoed through the crowded exhibit hall. The ceremony drove home Apple's message to the Mac software developers in attendance: drop whatever work you're doing in the old Mac OS and shift all your efforts to the operating system of the future.[9]

An often overlooked but important role of ceremony is to draw those from outside of the tribe into the tribe. Again, this is done at graduation ceremonies when parents, relatives, and friends are brought to the university to celebrate with graduates. In the workplace, it is typically believed that family and work should be separate. Therefore, workplace events should not be open to family. Yet, as discovered by an NHL Hockey coach I interviewed, negative impressions of the organization among players often have their genesis in the opinions and observations of girlfriends, spouses, moms and/or dads. To mitigate this, the organization actively includes parents, siblings, girlfriends, and spouses of the players in events that celebrate their role in the players' success. There is an important lesson here: ceremony can build key externalities to those that influence tribal members. Although it is most likely good policy to separate work from family in everyday tasks, sincerely reaching out to acknowledge those standing with members in their walk of life is important. One of my mother's most cherished possessions was her "Mistress of Patience in Husband Engineering Degree" given to her by Georgia Tech. It recognized her contributions as a spouse while my father obtained his Undergraduate Electrical Engineering Degree. Throughout her life, she was a bigger fan of the school than my dad!

Finally, rituals and ceremony provide needed confidence to take on tough challenges. The pep talk before a big game, touching a cherished icon before taking the field, locking arms and counting down, the Icelandic Skol Chant—these are all strong rituals that reduce stress, focus energy, and create zeal. Importantly, these are also rituals and celebrations that draw attention to and celebrate the collective not the individual.[10] Clearly, ceremony engages people around the things that matter most. We experience a sense of comfort and belonging. We are also reminded of values, responsibilities, experiences, and role models that define who we are and why we are on the journey. Although rituals require time, they are incredibly efficient in transforming self-doubt into a driving will to succeed. They can also be transformative as organizations pass from one stage to the next. While it is not efficient to celebrate everything, it is essential to celebrate the important things. It is also important to celebrate real milestones and realization of ambitious goals. The innovative organizations I observed and have been a part of, strike the right balance, highlighting the best aspects of the organization and its members without incurring celebration fatigue.

Storytelling

Closely tied to ceremony, storytelling is a primary means of creating common vision, common dialogue, and common knowledge within a tribe. Beyond data, information, charts, and facts, stories provide context, meaning, and application. From the beginning of time, stories have been the primary vehicle for capturing events and experiences that are then passed forward. Stories provide a greater boundary of understanding for what has happened, what is happening, and what might happen. These stories can be recollections of events or they can be myths and legends. In both instances, there is typically a hero, a journey, and a lesson learned. This progression is shaped by the storyteller and our own imagination. This is what makes them so compelling and useful. As illustrated in Figure 3.3, we can understand storytelling by examining the art of the story and the art of the storyteller.

There is no shortage of books, TED talks, and consulting reports about the characteristics of a good story. Among these works, one of the most popular themes is the approach of Disney and Pixar.[11] There are many good points and lessons in this approach, but it tends to co-mingle storytelling with the story itself. Of course, the two are intertwined in the context of a movie, but it is

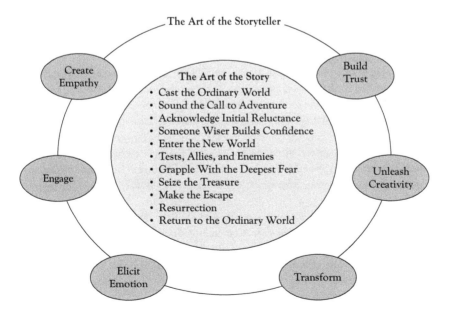

Figure 3.3: Stories and Storytellers

useful to untangle them to understand how storytelling is accomplished as a mechanism to transform and influence within an organization. Interestingly, much of the approach popularized by Pixar has its roots in myths, tales, and legends that were created by ancient tribes. The heart of these stories is captured in an incredible work by John Campbell, *The Hero with a Thousand Faces*. In this work, Campbell uncovers the central theme that underlies almost all tales of old.[12] This progression is also found in modern stories such as *Star Wars, Stranger Things*, and *Harry Potter*. It is a recipe that is compelling and can be applied to almost any context. I call this "the art of the story".

To illustrate the typical progression of myths and legends, I will use a story about one of my consulting/research projects. The goal is to illustrate the narrative building technique I discussed earlier in a fun and engaging way. Here goes,

> On a typical Sunday I was attending church with my wife. I was looking forward to having a scrumptious lunch after the service and then taking a hike around the lake. The hero (me) is cast in his ordinary world.
>
> As I was leaving the service the pastor pulled me aside and asked a favor. He wanted to know if I would be willing to consult with leaders of the denomination. The church was in trouble and needed my help. The call to adventure is sounded.
>
> I had never consulted with a church. I knew very little about the industry of religion and declined. The hero is reluctant and sees the challenge as troublesome.
>
> My wife, learning that I had declined, tells me that it would be a good and noble act of service to help the church. Perhaps it would atone for some my sins!. A wiser presence encourages and builds confidence.
>
> I meet with a council of Bishops but charge them nothing for my time or expenses. They describe a crisis. Declining attendance, the closing of churches, and dwindling financial support. They attribute this to changing society, lack of morals, media, and affluence; everything except the church itself. They are planning to launch an advertising campaign to bring the lost back to the church. The cost is millions of dollars. The Hero enters the new world.
>
> I ask them if I can test the assumption they are making and elevate the question. We need to determine if spirituality is really on the decline. The issue is bigger than the denomination and we are making assumptions without data. They politely fire me. The hero is tested.
>
> After a few weeks, as they are getting ready to write the check for the advertising campaign, they call me back and allow me to test the assumptions. After several rounds of survey, I discover that spirituality is on the rise! There are more people of faith now than in the past. Therefore, if there are more people of faith and traditional church attendance is falling, the question is, how are people exercising their faith? I am fired again. The hero grapples with deepest fear.
>
> Once again, I am called back. They are reluctant to purchase the advertising now that some doubt has been cast on their line of thinking. I am given a chance to investigate further.

I use narrative building to frame the bigger question of how someone of faith might worship. I use the dimensions of communion (what a person of faith seeks) and outreach (how a church gives to its community) for building narratives (see Figure 3.4). Further research strongly supports these narratives. There is a broader frontier of spirituality beyond the practices in traditional churches. I am fired again. The hero endures the supreme ordeal.

After some additional contemplation and some testimonies from leaders that are convinced by the narratives, the denomination accepts the narratives as true. They begin to see a larger world of faith around them and accept its legitimacy. I am asked to help them navigate this new frontier. The hero seizes the treasure.

After several meetings, the denomination is on a productive path. My time with them is ended. I decide that research and consulting within the context of religion is very difficult and, in the future, I will find other ways to atone for sin. The hero escapes.

I am changed by the experience. I learn that change happens over time and outside of formal meetings. I also learn it is possible to win a war even if you are losing all the battles. The hero experiences resurrection.

I go back to my church and listen to the sermon. I wonder how my church might change. I think about the lunch after the service and the walk around the lake. The hero returns to the ordinary world.

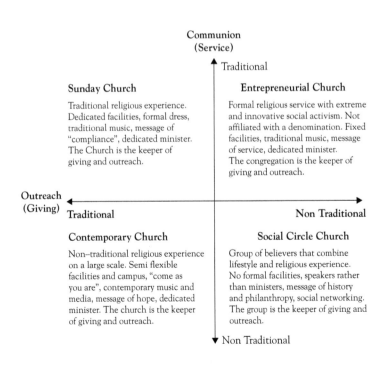

Figure 3.4: Spirituality and Religion: Possible Narratives

The power in this story form is its use of struggle and breakthroughs to solve extraordinary challenges. This is the heart of innovation and creativity. Although I did not pre-plan my story to follow the hero progression, its adherence to the form makes it a powerful mechanism for illustrating the technique of narrative building. It is one of my most popular stories and I get requests for it at many of my presentations. It is amazing to see how members of super projects use the same types of stories to bring life to complex data sets, pictures, images, and numerous complex problems. It is a creative form of data visualization. The myth can be used to tell the simplest comic book story, the most sophisticated drama, or to explain how something as sophisticated as gene editing occurs. When told with humor, twists, and insights, stories create lasting meaning, context, and a means of connecting. The myth is infinitely flexible, capable of endless variation without sacrificing any of its magic. Ironically, it outlives us all.

Great storytelling is at least as important as a great story. As illustrated, the storyteller must create empathy. The listener must be given a reason to "care" about the story and its characters. A good technique is to make the characters as much like the audience as possible. After all, we enjoy seeing ourselves in the story and relating to their plight. The storyteller must connect or engage the listener. This is done by making the story relevant and of value. Linking the story with a pressing issue or a needed lesson reminds the audience of the value to be gained. The storyteller must also elicit emotion. Through emphatic tone, humor, and other nonverbal cues, the audience can be drawn closer to the characters and stories' progression. Leaving a cliffhanger moment or building a "twist" in the tale draws out curiosity and an emotional stake in the characters. In a related manner, the listener should be transformed. A view might be changed, an assumption challenged, or a different perspective born. If the storyteller is really successful, then the listener's imagination becomes part of process which can unleash an important avenue of creativity. This is part of the magic of a Cirque Du Solei performance. The audience's imagination becomes part of the storytelling. Finally, the storyteller should create a bond of trust between themselves and the listener. The best mechanism for this is "believability" through the passion of performance. Because of the storyteller's zeal for telling the story, the audience begins to trust and bond with them, it seems like the story is only told to them because of the occasion or because they might be particularly receptive. Making the audience feel that they are the only ones hearing the tale is a hallmark of great storytelling and performance. It is the same magic that legendary performers such as Bruce Springsteen, U2, and The Rolling Stones have maintained for so long.

Loyalty

In today's world, loyalty may be the most elusive emergent structure to achieve; yet, it is critically important. In the context of tribalism, members are loyal to the tribe and the good of the tribe supersedes the good of an individual member. Loyalty brings out the very best in people's talents and skills. It also creates resolve and tenacity when times are the darkest. In fact, when recounting experiences and the times most cherished, many of my interviewees talked about the hardest times and the part of the journey when they were most sure that failure was at hand. To them, this was when loyalty was most important; it was also part of the legend of their work and experiences. Loyalty is also a key component of innovation. When we know that others "have our back", we are more likely to take chances, generate novel ideas, and communicate more honestly. In contrast, a lack of loyalty is a harbinger of suspicion, misinformation, and selfishness. The concept of loyalty is so powerful that "whistle-blowers" are typically not held in high esteem, even if they are right. If they are wrong, then the ostracization is even more intense, even if they had good intention. In a similar vein, betrayal is typically viewed as one of the most unforgivable transgressions in society. All this is to say that loyalty is powerful and must be managed carefully. The key is to create loyalty to the objective, to the values that guide behavior, to the integrity of the tools that accomplish work, and to each other. However, we do not want to create "blind loyalty" such that rogue actors emerge and an "echo chamber" is created that silences any contrary opinion. A tribe that creates this balance should not experience the "whistle-blower" or instances of dramatic betrayal. Again, it is difficult to achieve. Even the twelve disciples of Christ had trouble with the emergent structure of loyalty. Yet, it is something very noticeable in the extraordinary efforts of today's most innovative organizations.

Again, there are many books, articles, TED talks, and motivational speeches about the topic of loyalty. They all have something to offer, and some of these notions will appear in the descriptions to come. However, I witnessed and experienced a brand of loyalty that was bit different and perhaps more modern in the projects I observed. This perspective was also evident in the people I interviewed. The four key aspects of loyalty that were voiced consistently are: (1) *the right people*, (2) *collective individualism*, (3) *transparent communication*, and (4) *equity*.

Here is a very "hard" fact of life. Some people can only be truly loyal to their interests. There is a tendency in them to be selfish in framing the world around them and a blatant lack of concern for the interests of the organization or other members. As famously said by the character Annie Savoy in the movie *Bull Durham*, "*The world is made for people who aren't cursed with self-awareness.*"[13] I will leave it to psychologists to frame this personality type and its root causes. I will say that the most noticeable characteristic seems to be extreme zeal for their self-interest and extreme apathy for almost anything else. Yet, to those who frame the world this way, their self-interest is the best interest of the organization. Therefore, in their mind, they are the ultimate team players! Now, this is not to say that a person with extreme self-interest is not talented or needed. In contrast, they may be the most talented; after all, they have spent a lifetime honing only their skills and persona. It is to say that, in the long run, a collection of talents that work together as a group will typically outperform the super-talented, self-interested one. Fans of professional sports have seen this phenomenon for a long time. Yet, business professionals of sports teams cannot resist betting the franchise on the super-talented, super self-absorbed star. In achieving the extraordinary, the right people are empathetic, comfortable with the capabilities (and limitations) of their skills, polite, considerate, thoughtful, curious, and out to achieve something meaningful. They are also tolerant and very clever in effectively managing those that may not exhibit these characteristics. The main lesson is that a collection of the right talents and the right set of personality traits are the key to sustained success and bigger ideas. It is critical to achieving the right kind of loyalty.

So, with all of this discussion about organizations, tribes, and selflessness, does this imply that individuality and a "place in the sun" for individuals and their achievements is bad? NO! A big part of tribal spirit is the embrace and recognition that one is given by the tribe for a job well done. Even better is the recognition of a tribal member from those that are external to the tribe. Collective individualism is a structure that encourages individuality within the context of the collective. It is that moment when the most valuable player of a team recognizes that his/her achievements are the result of teammates and the encouragement of the fans. In contrast, it is not a tweet, action, or news conference that puts the focus on the individual and takes it away from the team and the task at hand. It allows a member to fully utilize their talents and enjoy some autonomy while working toward the goal of the collective. Again, this can be hard to manage. The line between individual behavior that boosts the collective and an act of rogue behavior is very thin. However, in very innovative organizations there is a strong sense of cultivating the innovative aspect of entrepreneurial activity with the rational responsibility of working within the collective.

Transparent communication forms a strong foundation for loyalty. In my own experiences in academe, I have received the e-mail explaining that a senior administrative person has resigned to devote time to their first love, research. It is a great story, but I know that the person was asked to step down and that there is now some chaos in the senior ranks. I also have a little less loyalty to the institution and those that lead it. Maybe it was better to communicate nothing at all, communicate in person, or just say there has been a change in leadership. Oddly enough, there seems to be an inverse correlation between transparent communication and adverse events. Not so in very innovate organizations, communication lanes are open and only facts are allowed to ride in both sunshine and rain. In addition, those communicating are accessible and visible. This is a phenomenon that is tough to initiate but equally tough to abandon once it is started. Honest communication is an acquired skill; it allows the tribe to correct the course, avoid surprises, and creatively seek solutions. This flow must be multi-way, from top to bottom, side to side, and bottom to top. Interestingly, many military generals, CEOs, and other leaders never knew their organizations were in trouble until it was too late. They were told exactly what they wanted to hear rather than what was actually happening. Aesop's fable about the emperor and his clothes is more than a story; it is a critical lesson in transparent communication.

Equity and consistency are critical to building loyalty. The literature in human resource management and organizational behavior is replete with first-class research on the importance of equity. Yet, it still seems difficult to define and even more difficult to achieve in practice. My research and experiences seem to indicate that equity is strongly dependent upon the first aspect of loyalty, finding the right people. Maybe, this is part of the mystery. If you have the wrong people, then you may never achieve a heathy threshold of equity. Therefore, there is no sense of loyalty. Yet, if you have the right people and they sense inequity, then they will likely find greener pastures. The magic seems to be creating a system of reward and progression that are based on key goals and developing the collective or the tribe. In concert, it is important to find the right people that will respond to the right incentives. It is similar to the push me–pull you of *Dr. Doolittle*. Both are connected and both must work together to achieve an objective. Companies such as Apple, Disney, SAS, and Cirque Du Solei are masters in building this structure of loyalty.

As evidenced by the amount of discussion, emergent structure is a very important aspect of building something beyond a team. To build it successfully is to set a strong predisposition for achieving something remarkable. Emergent structure exists between people, within groups of people, and between groups of people. It is an elusive concept because it is not something that is mandated or structured by organizational policy and procedure. It emerges over time; and it is shaped by the experiences, beliefs, and expectations of members. Viewing emergent structure from this lens is a way to assess its state and, if necessary, make needed repairs. Its absence can make the most talented individuals seem ordinary and underachieving. Its presence can leverage the talents of ordinary people, resulting in overachievement and incredible feats. A case in point is the journey of the Wright Brothers. Two ordinary bicycle makers achieve the feat of building the world's first flying machine. Competing teams, with greater talent and resources, failed at the same task. A huge part of the success was the emergent structure between the brothers, their helpers, and the people they met along the way. They leveraged their resources, moved forward through consensus, described the flight of birds through stories, celebrated victories, and exhibited loyalty to each other and those that helped them. The brothers demonstrated that ordinary people can accomplish the extraordinary when a tribal approach to innovation is present.

Notes

1. *ABC News*, "Kindergarten Handshake Ritual is Kids Favorite Part of the Day," May 30, 2018.
2. Carol Kinsey Goman, "Why IBM Brought Remote Workers Back to the Office-and Why Your Company Might be Next," *Forbes*, October 12, 2017.
3. S. G. Barsade, S. G. "The Ripple Effect: Emotional Contagion and Its Influence on Group Behavior," *Administrative Science Quarterly*, 47, 644–675, 2002.
4. Bill Murphy Jr., "7 Things Really Resourceful People Do," *Inc.*, March 28, 2014.
5. Leonard Mlodinow, *Elastic: Flexible Thinking in a Constantly Changing World*. Penguin Group, USA, 2019.
6. Jim Lovell and Jeffrey Kluger, *Lost Moon: The Perilous Voyage of Apollo 13*. Boston, MA: Houghton Mifflin Company. pp. 349–350, 1994.
7. John Markoff (December 11, 2015). "Artificial-Intelligence Research Center Is Founded by Silicon Valley Investors," *The New York Times*. Retrieved December 12, 2015.

8. Patti Sanchez, "Why Your Company Needs More Ceremonies," *Harvard Business Review*, July 27, 2016.
9. Phillip Michaels, "Jobs: OS 9 is Dead, Long Live OS X," *MacWorld*, May 1, 2002.
10. Paolo Guenzi, "How Rituals Effects Performance," *Harvard Business Review*, February 25, 2013.
11. Dean Movshovitz, *Pixar Storytelling: Rules for Effective Storytelling Based on Pixar's Greatest Films*. Bloop Animation Studios, 2nd edition, 2017.
12. Joseph Campbell, *The Hero with a Thousand Faces* (The Collected Works of Joseph Campbell). New World Library, 3rd edition, 2008.
13. David Rettwe, "The Wisdom of Bull Durham," *Psychology Today*, April 18, 2016

· 4 ·

ROLES AND RESPONSIBILITIES

Everybody is a genius. But if you judge a fish by its ability to climb a tree, it will live its whole life believing that it is stupid.

— Albert Einstein

A few years ago, I was conducting some research on unusual businesses. I was in South Africa visiting and experiencing cage diving tours with great white sharks. Basically, these tours take adventurers to where great whites swim, chum the water with blood, and then lower people (in steel cages) into the water for an up-close look. I was amazed as the captain asked the tourists to keep their hands in the cage during the dive. I asked him if any tourists had lost limbs on the adventure. He quickly replied, "*Yes! Sharks do not like to be petted*". Evidently, there is a strong urge to reach out and pet the sharks once you are among them. The captain then asked if I was ready to go on a cage dive. I immediately declined; I was there to observe. I was also there to explore the link between cage diving operations and the increase in shark attacks. I was no fan of the operation or of the fact that the South African government sanctioned the tours. The reaction bought me a lot of good-natured ridicule from the captain and some of the mates. "*Mr. College Professor, Mr. Brave American! Are you afraid of sharks!*" I looked at the captain and replied "*Not if they are on land. If they are on land and I have a baseball bat or club then they had better be afraid of me!*" As observed by Einstein, everybody is a genius in their proper context. It is a source of pride and an important form of identity.

Within the context of tribal innovation, the instinct of *Roles* and *Responsibility* is rooted in the role that members play in the journey and the ability to adapt swiftly to new roles when needed. I think I can speak for many people when I recall the times I have been part of a project team and was not sure why I was there or what I was expected to do. This is especially true in academia or in a church. In fact, I have been on some academic committees where consultants were hired to do the work we were tasked to do. I guess our collective role was to find someone else to solve the problem. Typically, when you are a part of meetings without focus or clear lines of responsibility, a leader will eventually emerge, make the problem small, and arrive at a quick solution (recall the chapter on ambition). Not to worry, as this goes on, you can spend the time drifting into a world or random thoughts. "*I wonder if vegetarians eat animal cookies?*" "*Isn't it cruel that packages which say "easy opening top" are the toughest to open?*" "*If you are scared half to death twice, do you die?*" "*How much time did that guy spend learning that pencil trick?*" "*If you rip a hole in a net then there are fewer holes.*" You get the idea. For all of us, being part of a project without a clearly defined role and responsibility is an invitation to drift into the world of stranger things. In tribes, everyone has a role that is important and synergistic with their talents. There is no time for random thoughts because during the time spent in a meeting or out of the meeting, the tribe is counting on you to fulfil a responsibility.

There are three important aspects associated with the assignment of roles and responsibilities: (1) defining the critical roles needed for the tribe to succeed, (2) matching the talent, capabilities, and interests of members to roles, and (3) coordinating sets of activities across roles. It is also important for the tribe to take on an identity. Similar to a professional sports team, all members play a primary role, can take on another role if needed, and are all bonded by the logo, colors, and mascot that seal the identity. When all this happens successfully, you belong, you contribute, you coordinate, and you are quite likely to achieve. Let's take a look at each of these dimensions.

Critical Roles

Roles within tribes are legendary. Some of these roles include chief (leadership), elders (wisdom), hunters (sustenance), skinners (materials), and shaman (medicine). These roles have been compared to the social tasks that are needed and frequently occur within start-ups.[1] However they are defined, roles describe the way a group works together and how each individual behaves, contributes, and relates to others. Knowing the various roles and who holds them is key in managing expectations, building trust, and creating critical channels of communication. In some group contexts, these roles may be combined into a single role and attributed to the leader. This "messiah" model is found throughout military, autocratic business organizations, religion, and some governmental organizations. It is an attractive model. Nothing inspires us more than the thought of a magnanimous leader that seems to know the future and can navigate us to the promised land. This is true within a project team or in a major business organization. However, it is highly unlikely that anyone can be good at every critical role and also manage them all simultaneously. Therefore, it is important to "unpack" the roles that are typically bundled in magnanimous leadership and distribute them to the people most able to perform them effectively. While doing this, it is important to redefine the role of leadership. Tribal history and the organizational style of modern-day super projects seem to echo this sentiment.

So, what are the roles that are critical within a project? A starting point on this quest is to determine what behaviors are critical for group success. In the 1970s, Dr. Meredith Belbin and his research team at Henley Management College began observing teams to discover factors that distinguish high performance from low performance.[2] The research revealed that the difference between success and failure for a team was not dependent on factors such as the intellect of individual team members, but more on the behavior of those individuals. Belbin and his team began to identify separate clusters of behavior, each of which formed distinct team contributions or "team roles." They defined a team role as: "A tendency to behave, contribute and interrelate with others in a particular way." Belbin's work uncovered nine archetypal team roles, all of which have essential parts to play in successful teamwork over time. These roles are:

Cerebral Roles

Plant: Creative, imaginative, unorthodox. Solves difficult problems. Excusable weaknesses: Ignores incidentals. Too preoccupied to communicate effectively.

Monitor Evaluator: Sober, strategic, and discerning. Sees all options. Judges accurately. Excusable weaknesses: Lacks drive and ability to inspire others.

Specialist: Single-minded, self-starting, and dedicated. Provides knowledge and skills in rare supply. Excusable weaknesses: Contributes on only a narrow front. Dwells on technicalities.

Action Roles

Shaper: Challenging, dynamic, and thrives on pressure. The drive and courage to overcome obstacles. Excusable weaknesses: Prone to provocation. Offends people's feelings.

Implementer: Disciplined, reliable, conservative, and efficient. Turns ideas into practical actions. Excusable weaknesses: Can be inflexible. Slow in responding to new possibilities.

Completer Finisher: Painstaking, conscientious, and anxious. Searches out errors and omissions. Delivers on time. Excusable weaknesses: Inclined to worry unduly. Reluctant to delegate.

People Roles

Coordinator: Mature, confident, and a good chairperson. Clarifies goals, promotes decision-making, and delegates well. Excusable weaknesses: Can be seen as manipulative. Offloads personal work.

Team Worker: Co-operative, mild, perceptive, and diplomatic. Listens, builds, and averts friction. Excusable weaknesses: Indecisive in crunch situations.

Resource Investigator: Extrovert, enthusiastic, and communicative. Explores opportunities. Develops contacts. Excusable weaknesses: Over-optimistic. Loses interest once initial enthusiasm has passed.

Belbin's framework provides a nice context for understanding roles as behaviors that lead to extraordinary performance. It also aligns well with the roles of ancient tribes. The elder matches the Belbin's role of the plant. The shaman is the specialist. The primary warrior is the shaper. The chief is the coordinator. A tribal judge is the monitor evaluator. The spiritual guide is the team worker. The tribal skinner is the completer finisher. While these matches are my own observation and there is room for refinement, the point is that these behaviors are shaped as formal roles that are identifiable and distributed in such a way that the tribe is predisposed to function at its most effective level.

Within the projects examined in my research, roles are very prominent; and while matching the general framework of Belbin, they are a bit more defined and a lot more creative. Themes that give definition to the roles are based on everything from science fiction movies (*The Matrix, Star Wars, Star Trek*), fantasy novels (*Harry Potter, Lord of the Rings, Story of Fire and Ice*), and comic book heroes (Watchmen, Avengers, Justice League) to characters found in video gaming (League of Legends, World of Warcraft). No matter how they are identified, the roles are those deemed essential by members in coordinating and moving the tribe toward its destination. There are a few other distinguishing features of the roles. First, the role a member adopts is a *primary* role. It is possible to adopt a secondary role. This is actually encouraged to build "reserve" talent in case of unexpected changes within the tribe. Second, a member can participate in the execution of all roles. One is never fully restricted to a particular playground; if someone has a contribution beyond their role, it is encouraged. However, the member is responsible for the execution of their primary role. Third, a member can switch roles if there are problems or an unexpected lack of fit. It is not encouraged but it is better than rigidly adhering to role dysfunction. Finally, an observation, if an important responsibility is not assigned as a role, it will typically not get done. Therefore, it is critically important to establish roles and responsibilities before you launch a project. Imagine a sports team that defines and assigns responsibilities as the game is played. Only extreme luck, or an opponent that assigns no roles, would allow the team to prevail. Highlighted in Figure 4.1 are some

Cerebral
___

> Architect: Provides leadership, vision, coaching, and direction.
>
> Wizard: Provides research, data, scientific experiments.
>
> Oracle: Provides expertise in critical subject matter.

Action
___

> Flamekeeper: Keeps track of time, finds resources, schedules.
>
> Rainmaker: Boundary spanner, finds unconventional paths, networks.
>
> Author/Historian: Transfer ideas to words and words into stories and documents.
>
> Artist: Transfers ideas to art. Creates visuals, charts, illustrations.

People
___

> Facilitator: Stages formats of discussion, referees, negotiates, reasons.
>
> Seeker: Roams among other teams. Gives and receives information & knowledge.
>
> The Voice: Transfers ideas through the spoken word. Speaks on behalf of the Tribe.

Figure 4.1: A Sample of Key Roles and Responsibilities in Super Projects

of the most colorful, impactful, and common roles I have observed in research and in experience. They are mapped to Belbin's behavioral archetypes.

The cerebral roles and responsibilities address the activity of critical thinking. Are we addressing the right question? Have we localized the problem? Have we identified the right sequence of cause and effect? Have we drifted away from the problem? What is fact? What is conjecture? To me, this is the hallmark of modern leadership. Yet, it can be found in the activities of ancient tribes. The architect is responsible for providing the vision, coaching, and direction needed to achieve the tribal goal. It is a role that demands a lot of presence, ambition, experience, listening, and patience. The architect accomplishes the role by "walking around" and asking questions. This is not a new idea, but it has been lost with the emergence of e-mails, PowerPoints, and telework.[3] To be present and to be engaged as an architect is to signal importance and concern. It also builds a strong disposition for positive emergent structure. It is not enough to have an open-door policy. You must ask tribal members to open their doors to you.

The wizard is typically the role I have played on projects. I love the role, I am qualified for the role, and I have done very well in the role. However, I also have a strong sense of curiosity and I love to be around people. The wizard's life can be very solitary from time to time. Therefore, I have sometimes asked to be seeker (discussed in a little while) where I can roam among other tribes and learn what they are doing. I have always been denied the request. I was told that I like to talk too much, tell stories, and would have trouble returning to my tribe with the knowledge I have collected, probably true. The wizard is responsible for science and fact checking. Data, experiments, surveys, the latest articles, seminars, and conferences are the playing fields. Data and research are authenticated, filtered, and organized so that the tribe has the best set of facts and the best science available for consideration. It takes a heart for science, a curious mind, and a deep knowledge of the tools of statistics. However, this does not necessarily imply that a Ph.D. is required. Wilbur Wright played the role of wizard in the invention of the flying machine. He had a knack for experimentation and a devotion to the scientific method as a means of discovery. Wilbur was self-educated in science and sharpened his engineering skills, building bicycles in the family business. His highest educational credential was a high school diploma. The main lesson is not to "guess" about science, data, and information. Make it a role and responsibility and assign it to someone that is science minded and on a quest for the truth.

The oracle, sometimes called "the genius", is a person that can give wise and authoritative knowledge. In many contexts, this role is given to someone that is not a member of the tribe. It may be an outside expert or a consultant that has subject matter knowledge of some aspect of the project. The role may also be assigned to someone within the organization but who is working on a different project with a different tribe. I have played this role a few times for research teams seeking grants from the National Science Foundation or the Defense Research Projects Agency. Typically, a research team will be told by a reviewer that they need additional subject matter expertise to win a grant. I will be called upon to play that role and be a permanent part of the research project or just a temporary resource. It is a fun role to play, and the major requirement is to provide focused expertise while helping to shape the bigger picture. This is similar to Belbin's "specialist" role, and it is critical to know when the limits of a team's knowledge have been reached and that an oracle is required. The motion picture *The Matrix* demonstrates these important aspects of the role. The name, as used by some of the projects researched, is a nod to the movie's character.

Action-oriented roles are the "icebreakers" of getting things done. They remove obstacles, find paths, document findings, and keep the work on track. The flamekeeper is tasked with managing the time and resources of the project. Scheduling, tracking time, tracking resources, and finding resources are the responsibilities of this role. The flamekeeper can be thought of as the source of rationality and accountability within the tribe. They also take on the responsibility of a quartermaster, finding and allocating resources as needed. Again, there are people who are incredible in this role. Attention to detail, a process mindset, a sense of time, a knack for provisioning, and the ability to administer a gentle "nudge" are the requirements.

The rainmaker is an interesting role and responsibility. This person is responsible for boundary spanning, finding unconventional paths, and networking within the organization. A rainmaker knows everyone and knows where to seek the unconventional. They have a passion for building and growing relationships. In some sense, it is similar to the "fixer" that is popularized in mobster movies. Someone who can clean up a mess or find avenues to do what seems to be impossible. I once worked in a fascinating project for the J4 staff of the Department of Defense. The goal was to identify supply routes for U.S. forces that were deep in the country of Iraq. We came up with some very innovative ideas. However, they were rejected by leadership as "unlawful" and costly even if they were possible. Immediately, our tribe called upon the rainmaker to investigate the claims. This person knew lawyers, legislators, flag officers, and almost everyone in the Pentagon. The rainmaker quickly determined that the concerns were not valid. The supply routes were not forbidden by law and not very costly. Plus, they could be established very quickly. He also discovered other supply routes that were unconventional and effective. None of this would have been possible without this role. A typical group would have stopped at the first push back and an innovation opportunity would have been lost.

The artist and author/historian can be discussed together. They perform essentially the same responsibility just in a different medium. The author transfers ideas to words while the artist transfers ideas to art. First, let's say that they are among the most important roles. An idea is only actionable if it can be communicated from one person or group to another. The process of idea capture, whether in word or in art, helps to refine the idea. It also subjects the notion to its first proof of concept. Second, the skill set and disposition for these roles typically require something beyond formal training and education. It seems to be an innate skill. A level of creativity is required in this role that is difficult to describe but obvious when it is in action. Simplicity seems to be part of this skill. An artist or author should be able to capture ideas in a form that is not tedious or distracting. Engagement is another aspect of the transfer. Artwork and written words should engage the audience and elicit discussion, debate, and ideas for further steps. Playfulness is also part of the mix. Humor, color, pictures, analogies, twists, and interactivity all help create an experience that captures the work while keeping the gates of imagination and creativity open.

The final set of roles are rooted in the interactions of people. The facilitator is the peacemaking role of the tribe. This person stages formats of discussion, referees, and makes sure that every voice is heard and counted. The best-known tribal incarnation of this task is the "talking stick". Also known as a "speaker's staff", this carved wooden staff was an instrument of aboriginal democracy used by many tribes, especially those located along the Northeast Coast of North America. The talking stick was passed among the group as a means of recognizing an individual's right to speak. It was also used by leaders as a symbol of their authority and right to speak in public.[4] The facilitator is responsible for being the living, breathing talking stick of the group. This can be a tough task, but there are people who have enormous talent in this regard. They tend to be observers, note takers, acute listeners, and masters of equity within the organization. Those trained in human resource management tend to excel in this role. Notice also that this role is separated from the cerebral roles. As noted earlier, it is important to unbundle roles that are typically bundled into the leader's role. This is the most important role to unbundle. Leaders, typically occupying one or more of the cerebral roles, love the talking stick. It is important that they do not get too much time in its company.

The seeker is the knowledge gateway from one tribe to another. The responsibility of this person is to visit other tribes. Bringing knowledge to their discussions and bringing back knowledge to their "home" tribe. There are two significant contributions of the seeker. First, there is a leveraging effect. The seeker can leverage knowledge created by one group to help the efforts of another group. This is true even if there is no knowledge to report. While working on a cybersecurity project for DARPA, our seeker visited other groups that were working on similar projects throughout the Department of Defense. When she returned to our group for a report-out, only one PowerPoint slide was presented. It read, "They are as lost as we are!" We eventually found our way as did other tribes, but it was good to know that we were not the only one struggling in the beginning. The second effect is efficiency. In large organizations, it is likely that efforts, experiments, and information are duplicated. The seeker can identify existing and potential redundancies saving the organization's time and money. Seekers tend to be curious, extraverted, loaded with initiative, and able to communicate. They also know that it is important to not get distracted and report back to their home tribe. For this reason, I will likely not be a seeker although I would love to give it a try.

The voice is the role and responsibility of presenting the findings, conclusions, and recommendations of the tribe to outsiders. They also capture and interpret the feedback they receive. Again, notice this is not automatically tied to the leadership role. It can be part of the leadership role but it is not required to be so. In some sense, this can be thought of as the ambassador or diplomat of the tribe. Professionalism, knowledge, empathy, presence, improvisation, humor, the ability to gather feedback, and stellar communication skills are the main requirements. The main goal is to ensure that the tribe's voice is heard accurately and effectively in a presentation setting. In the best cases, the voice knows when and where other members should carry part of the presentation, when no presentation is needed, and how to integrate the tribe's presentation with the presentations of other tribes. Of course, the voice works closely with the holders of other roles, particularly the artist, in shaping the message and presentation for external audiences.

Matching Talent with Roles

A very important, yet, tricky aspect of this task is matching the role with the prevailing talent of the member. In some instances, a member may view themselves as perfect for a particular role when, in reality, another role is best suited for their talents. I remember auditioning for my elementary school's production of "*The Frog Princess*". I wanted to be the Prince. The Prince would accompany the Princess, wear a sword, and wear a cool cape. The Princess would undoubtedly be played by "the girl" that I and every boy in school had the biggest crush on. I tried very hard to get the part. I sang, I danced, and I left it all on the stage. However, I did not sound like a Prince, I was not as tall as a Prince, and let's face it, there were other guys that looked more like a Prince than me. I saw the final roster and did not see my name listed as Prince. Worse than that, I was not a fan of the guy who got the part. I walked home terribly disappointed but quickly moved on to reading comic books and doing homework. Later that afternoon, I heard the phone ring and heard my mom talking in an animated fashion. She bolted into the den where I was reading the latest Ironman comic and told me that I was expected at the rehearsal for The Frog Prince. I had been cast in the role of the Frog! Well, if you know the story, the Frog plays a major part and gets a kiss from the Princess. It turns out the Prince does not get a kiss. Not what I had initially hoped for in a role, but it was very cool. I was the best Frog I could be. I still get compliments on the performance. The moral is that every role is important and that there is glory in playing the Frog as well as the Prince. Sometimes, there is more glory in being the Frog. In one of the projects I observed, there was a group of computer programmers called the "blue collar immortals". They took turns bringing an old steel lunch pail to the lab. The pail represented their "blue collar" contribution to the project and their devotion to taking care of the tedious coding details that would make others cringe. They were a proud bunch and very happy to be Frogs. It was a badge of honor.

It is also possible that once a role is assigned, it becomes obvious that the desired match does not exist. If you have been in academe long enough, you will experience this phenomenon a few times. It is typically found in the appointment of a stellar academic to a deanship. In the corporate world, the same thing happens when a person is promoted to a level of incompetence; it is known as the Peter Principle. In contrast, when a person holding a role seems to accomplish his/her responsibilities effortlessly, then there is evidence of desired fit. If there is an obvious lack of fit, it is a mistake to think the person will grow into the role or that things will magically get better over time. This only frustrates the person in the ill-fitting role as well as those people in roles that are aligned with their skills. This rapid response was observed in most of the teams I studied. It was amazing how quickly these mismatches were resolved without conflict or disruption. Most often, the mismatch is noted by the member themselves and roles are recast accordingly. These were rare cases as careful thought and attention was given to the assignment of roles. Finally, to reiterate, it is very desirable for members to play a few roles when needed. It is also possible that a role is only needed for certain parts of the project and will come and go as needed. This aspect of role adaptability among members as well as recurring and non-recurring roles allows the tribe to adapt.

There are wonderful tools and techniques for matching talent with roles. Belbin's framework provides a behavioral basis for creating this alignment. The Margerison-McCann Team Management Profile is a tool that can help match skills with potential roles. Using a set of 60 questions, this profile establishes baseline information about each member's traits and work preferences. These work preferences provide insight into an individual's interpersonal and team-building skills, their organizing and decision-making abilities, and their leadership strengths. Their archetypes are:

• **Reporter-Adviser:** Supporter, helper, tolerant, a collector of information, knowledgeable, flexible, dislikes being rushed.

• **Creator-Innovator:** Imaginative, future-oriented, enjoys complexity, creative, likes research work.

• **Explorer-Promoter:** Persuader, "seller," easily bored, influential, outgoing, likes varied, exciting, stimulating work.

• **Assessor-Developer:** Analytical and objective, developer of ideas, experimenter, enjoys prototype or project work.

• **Thruster-Organizer:** Organizes and implements, quick to decide, results-oriented, sets up systems, analytical.

• **Concluder-Producer:** Practical, production-oriented, likes schedules and plans, takes pride in reproducing goods and services, values effectiveness and efficiency.

• **Controller-Inspector:** Strong on control, detail-oriented, low need for people contact, an inspector of standards and procedures.

• **Upholder-Maintainer:** Conservative, loyal, supportive, personal values important, strong sense of right and wrong, work motivation based on purpose.

Along with work preferences, behaviors, and traits, roles can be based on personality profiles, past experiences, preferences, and peer suggestion. However, based on my observations, these forms of assessment may miss some key aspects of skill and disposition needed to effectively perform a role. Especially if the goal is ambitious, the tribe is eclectic, and the context is driven by discovery, invention, and problem solving. There is a lack of playfulness in these approaches and a potential for politics to outweigh collective interests. As implemented by a few teams, a great first step might be to have members take a few tests that match them to movie stars, a member of the Beatles, or other aspects of "pop culture". There are several of these non-scientific tests that can begin a basis of discussion about role fit and "break the ice" in terms of placing members in roles. Importantly, precision is not the goal; it is assigning primary responsibility for the fulfillment of the role to an able member. In a few teams, members were first sorted into the "Hogwarts Houses" of Gryffindor, Hufflepuff, Ravenclaw, and Slytherin as featured in the *Harry Potter* fantasy novels.[5] These houses are described in Figure 4.2. This provided an initial, and incredibly accurate, read of personality characteristics that might lead to greater success in a tribal role.

Gryffindors were noted to be very strong in the role of wizard, genius, and seeker. Slytherins seem suited for architects and seekers. Hufflepuffs tend to

The Houses of Hogwarts

Hogwarts is a fictional British school of magic for students aged eleven to eighteen, and is the primary setting for J. K. Rowling's Harry Potter series. Hogwarts is divided into four houses, each bearing the last name of its founder. Students are assigned to their house by the Sorting Hat.

Gryffindor:
Values courage, bravery, nerve and chivalry.

Slytherin:
Values ambition, cunning, leadership, and resourcefulness.

Ravenclaw:
Values intelligence, creativity, learning, and wit.

Hufflepuff:
Values hard work, patience, justice, and loyalty.

Figure 4.2: *Harry Potter*: The Houses of Hogwarts for Assigning Roles

be strong as flamekeepers, authors, and facilitators. Ravenclaws show strength as artists, authors, and genius. I suggested using the Pottermore test to a Two Star General in the U.S Army as a way to align skills and behaviors with roles. I told him that I had taken the test (Gryffindor) and been assigned a role in a project based on the result. I also told him that I used the test in consulting projects to establish teams and that the results were fantastic. It really works! His enthusiasm was quite a bit less than mine. Something like a blank stare. However, he returned to his command, read the first *Harry Potter* book (he had no clue who Harry Potter was), and then gave it a try. Not only did he become a fan of *Harry Potter*, he was completely amazed by the improvement in his team's performance. They became more tribal and took on greater challenges with ease. I asked him if he had taken the test: he had, and was classified as Slytherin. I suggested he visit Harry Potter World and get a Slytherin Wizard's Cloak and a wand. The cloak looks much cooler than army dress uniforms. Again, I got the blank stare; I don't think it will happen. Anyway, this is a creative way to develop roles that keep the task fun but also enlighten members about their predispositions for success. Together, formal behavioral frameworks and creative techniques can provide a broader perspective of a person's work preference and a more engaging process. The end result should be a "seating" of roles and responsibilities such that they are understood, valued, and managed effortlessly by their owners.

Find Your Identity

A final aspect of roles and responsibilities that must be acknowledged is role *cohesion* and *identity*. If there is harmony between people and their roles, then there must also be harmony across the roles. The first bridge to cross in that quest is the correct identification of needed roles. It is likely unwise to place a banjo player in a jazz band. Likewise, a saxophone player probably has nothing to add to a folk band. When you have the right combination of roles, then the tribe takes on cohesion and an identity. That is the final piece of the roles and responsibility quest. Within the context of music, the band takes on a sound and vibe that is identifiable. Within a Broadway play, the story takes on a context and progression that is driven by the interplay of roles. Within a sports team, there is a way of playing and sometimes a swagger that reflects the assigned roles and the shared record of success. The key question to ask is *"What must happen for us to achieve success?"* The next step is to determine what underlying roles are needed to support that sequence and where role "breakdowns" might damage the overall progress. I asked a well-known professional football coach about cohesion, critical roles, and breakdowns. He had a very interesting perspective on the subject. To him, the most critical role on a football team is the long snapper. This is the person that "hikes" the football to the punter for kicking the ball back to the opponent. The long snapper also "hikes" the ball to the placeholder for field goals and extra-points. Without someone effective in that role, then there is no field position. There is also no confidence in scoring within the opponent's side of the field or after a touchdown. The game becomes very different and difficult. There is also no rhythm in the game. The uncertainty of transferring the ball to the kicker damages the flow of the game and puts undue pressure on other role-players. Although the long snapper is unheralded, rarely wins a most valuable player trophy, and is never featured in interviews after the game, the role is crucial in linking the more high-profile roles of the team. It is time to recognize the outstanding long snappers of football and those that play similar roles within any organization!

The second bridge to cross is giving the group a visible *identity*. I have worked with project teams in the Department of Defense for many years. These teams are assigned problems or challenges to solve with a big emphasis on thinking innovatively. It is a part of my career that I enjoy. However, when I first started this work, teams were numbered (team 1, team 2, etc.) and there were no roles. They basically took the problem statement and went into a workspace to begin solving the challenge. They immediately began looking for the quickest way out of the assignment. The most innovative thing they did was list ideas on a chart in hopes of finding something to call the task complete. I was amazed by this given that my experiences with projects and problem solving were quite different. It was also ironic because these very smart men and women had strong tribal instincts and strong identity within their respective services. However, all of that was lost when the task was set up in this manner. The first thing I did was give each group a name. I am a big fan of NHL Hockey (go Carolina Hurricanes!), so I assigned each group a team that was near their home base. Now team 1 was the Boston Bruins, team 2 was the Chicago Blackhawks, etc. Doing this gave them a different context of who they were and who other teams were. In other words, we have added *identity* to the mix. There are team colors, there are team mascots, and there is a feeling of belonging. A few members told me that their favorite hockey team was assigned to another group; yet, they became a fan of their assigned hockey team because it bonded the members in that context. There is a lot of power in giving a group a sense of identity through adoption of a team name, team colors, and a team logo. I am still amazed at the difference a dose of identity makes in connecting members and instilling a sense of collective pride.

In sum, it is important for organizations to establish well-defined roles that are derived from assessment of behaviors, work preferences, and traits. It is also important to add a touch of creativity and fun in identifying these roles. There should be harmony between the owner of a role and his/her responsibilities. Force fitting a person to a role or hoping for some miracle adaptation is not encouraged. Allowing someone to grow into a role is encouraged; there is a difference. There should be cohesion across roles. The interplay between roles is critical and points of potential breakdown must be identified. These points of breakdown may not be in the glamorous or high-profile roles (e.g. the Quarterback); they may arise in the less glamorous roles and responsibilities (e.g. the Long Snapper). Finally, a sense of identity adds a level of connectedness and *esprit de corps* that reinforces role of ownership and pride of craftsmanship. Taken together, these elements set the stage for greater coordination and greater accomplishment.

Notes

1. J. Greathouse, "Are you a Business Shaman, Skinner or Hunter?," *Forbes*, June 4, 2016.
2. Meredith R. Belbin, *Management Teams: Why They Succeed or Fail.* Oxford: Butterworth-Heinemann, 2003.
3. Henry Mintzberg, *Simply Managing: What Managers Do—and Can Do Better.* Berrett-Koehler Publishers, 1st edition, September 2, 2013.
4. Edwin L. Wade, The Arts of the North American Indian: Native Traditions in Evolution. Hudson Hills, 1995.
5. The Sorting Hat—Pottermore, https://www.pottermore.com/writing-by-jk-rowling/the-sorting-hat

· 5 ·

TRUST

Courage is what it takes to stand up and speak; courage is also what it takes to sit down and listen.

— Winston Churchill

Trust may be the most difficult tribal instinct to tangibly capture in description, but it is also a unique bond that holds a tribe together, particularly, in the very toughest times. As noted in Churchill's quote, it is the courage to speak and the courage to listen. This is most likely to occur in a context where one feels safe and supported in both rain and shine. That context has to be predictable, reliable, and reciprocal for all members of the tribe. When there is a strong presence of trust, an organization will almost never lapse into chaos or disarray. Instead, when times are toughest, tightly connected groups tend to become more resilient and more egalitarian and develop a greater bond that is built on mutual trust.

In World War II, England braced for aerial bombardments intended to cause mass hysteria and break the spirits of its citizens. The Churchill government was worried that people would move into bomb shelters and never move out. These shelters might also become a breeding ground for discontent, criminal activity, and espionage. To the surprise of the British government, the complete opposite occurred; throughout the Blitz, the people of London went to work, returned to shelters in an orderly manner, and adopted codes of conduct (emergent structure) to deal with the chaos. Sharing resources, caring for others, and credibly communicating amongst each other created the tribal instinct of trust that allowed Londoners to endure a campaign of bombing that was more intense than that found on the battlefield.[1]

We learn trust at an early age, often from experience. As a young boy, I would often accompany my uncles and grandfather on hunting trips. Sometimes we would go hunting for raccoons. While cute, a raccoon will destroy a field of corn. So, it is sometimes necessary to decrease the population. These hunts occur in winter, late at night, and in muddy fields that are in the middle of nowhere. You release the dogs; they chase the raccoon up the tree and you "take care" of the racoon with a shotgun. One very cold night we were hunting in a field that was very unfamiliar to us. The land had lots of old barbed wire fences, streams, and other obstacles. However, we had a guide, Mr. Kelly. He was an older gentleman, chewed tobacco, used filthy language, and was not exactly physically fit. My grandfather told us to take him along and trust him; he knew the land very well. All during the hunt my uncles and I talked about how we wanted to ditch the old man, Kelly. He was slow, talked all the time, and made fun of us. Suddenly, we heard a screech at the edge of the woods that was horrifying. We shined a light toward the noise; it was a pack of angry bobcats. These are animals that are mean and do not like to be disturbed. Once the bobcats saw the light, they charged. Mr. Kelly yelled to us, "*FOLLOW ME!*" Instead, we dropped our flashlights and ran like hell. We ran through a few streams, tracked through mud, jumped, and fell across fences. We seemed to be running in circles. We finally found our way back to the main house. We were out of breath, covered in mud, wet, and bleeding from the barbed wire and thorns of the bushes we had run through. We looked back toward the fields and woods we had just crossed. My Uncle Randy asked, *I wonder what happened to old man Kelly?* I said, *The bobcats probably got him. Poor soul, he deserved better.* Suddenly, we hear a voice ring out from the darkness of the front porch. "*What took you boys so long?*" It was Mr. Kelly, not a drop of mud on him, no sign of exhaustion, standing there with a cold can of beer. He knew the short cut, he knew bobcats would not chase you for long, and he knew where the truck was parked. It was a lesson in trust. Sometimes the most trustworthy person may be a troll like Mr. Kelly, not a movie star, star athlete, or yourself.

So, how can trust be framed so that it is something we can diagnose and perhaps treat within an organization? There are two interconnected aspects that seem very important. First, there is the overall context or "standard" of trust. This is the landscape or culture of trust within an organization and how it manifests itself in principles or standards. It is based on behavior, ethics, expectations, and codes of conduct that may not be formalized in words but are well known in action. It is similar to the aspects of emergent structure discussed before but different because it involves deeper aspects of a relationship between members as well as the relationship between the organization and its members. These relationships are built over time through experiences. The second aspect is the manifestation of trust within a tribe. That is very simply the exchange of knowledge. Organizations with high thresholds of trust will create and share knowledge seamlessly. This flow is a manifestation of the standard of trust and provides the fuel necessary for the best ideas and the best innovative outcomes.

The Standard of Trust

An effective standard of trust among a group of people is built through actions, experiences, the test of trying times, as well as the test of the best of times. It is part of the fabric that connects people; and it is something that, when maliciously broken, is almost impossible to completely repair. Of course, there are many academic studies and consulting frameworks that capture this concept in many different ways. In a prior piece of research, I used many of these ideas to build a definition of trust between an organization and its shareholders.[2] The context I examined was the digital communication of corporate crisis to shareholders (employees, customers, and shareholders). It was interesting to find that the standard of trust within the organization was a very accurate predictor of the effectiveness of communication.[3] In other words, receivers of the communication were able to sense the trustworthiness of the organization through their digital communications. This trustworthiness was not "baked" into the communication. Instead, effective organizations had strong standards of trust that was reflected in their communications. These standards of trust are also found in very innovative organizations as well as the amazing tribes of old. As illustrated in Figure 5.1, these dimensions are: *credibility, efficacy, resolve, consistency, commitment,* and *accountability*. This framework embodies aspects of *strategic trust* (trust in leadership), *personal trust* (trust in each other), and *organizational trust* (trust in the organization).[4] It should also be viewed as a chronology of trust: actions of the past, present, and future. This

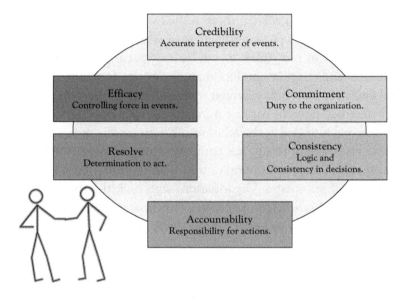

Figure 5.1: Standards of Trust

provides a perspective that is grounded in both experiences and expectations. Ideally, there is a strong history of trust and a strong expectation that these standards will guide the tribe in the future.

Credibility

Within the context of tribal innovation, organizational credibility is the accurate interpretation and communication of data, information, and knowledge. Concepts such as honesty, genuineness, and integrity are part of this construct. A lack of credibility is one the hardest obstacles for an organization to overcome. An organization can be forgiven for many things, but a lack of honesty is a stigma that is hard to shed. Honest workers will select themselves out of organizations that lack credibility and find refuge in firms with values more consistent with their own. It will also be hard to recruit the best thinkers and innovators. Research has shown that such people are mostly motivated by an organization's values and purpose.[5] Within the organizations and super projects of my research, three main themes capture the notion of credibility: (1) *knowing things as they really are*, (2) *quickly communicating what we know honestly*, and (3) *communicating the important things we know to those who need to know*. In a sense, it is a collective understanding and "way" of working in which value is placed on facts, established cause and effect, and honest observation. Conjecture, partial information, inference, and wishful thinking are very hesitantly invented or communicated. If they are part of a discussion, great effort is made to note that the conversation has progressed beyond the boundary of fact and data. Rapid, fluid, and accurate communication of facts and events is practiced throughout the organization to fight off speculation and rumor. This extends to personnel announcements, budget information, parking, and even the menu at the cafeteria. However, this does not imply that there is a flood of unbridled information flowing within the organization. Too much information, without a method to organize and prioritize it, harms credibility. Important information can easily hide in the tsunami of everyday communication. Members can also feel overwhelmed or fatigued by constant communication. The magic is creating flows of data, information, and knowledge that are accurate, prioritized, and readily accessible to those who need it most.

Efficacy

The University of North Carolina at Chapel Hill (UNC) is a fairly tribal organization. There is a "Carolina Way" of positive ethics, community, and values that seem to distinguish us as an organization. We have a long history and a tradition of excellence. However, the university also had an artifact of history that became very divisive and tested our sense of connectedness. The object was a statue of a confederate soldier that stood at the main lawn of the campus. Erected in the early 1900s, the monument became more divisive as the years rolled by. Protests emerged and calls for action became louder from those who supported and those who opposed the monument. The chancellor of the university made it clear that she opposed symbols that might cause division. She also noted that she was not able to do anything about the statue. State law as well as rules and procedures made it impossible to act. Of course, this only enraged those on both sides of the issue.[6] This is an example of very poor organizational efficacy. If an organization is not a controlling force in events, then trust is broken within the organization and between the organization and other constituencies. Yet, saying "it is out of our control" is a very tempting tact for leaders and organizational members to take when times get tough. Organizations can lose control of their destiny due to budget constraints, competitors, regulatory penalties, shifting winds of management, or the inability to understand their environment. If this happens, it is critically important to quickly regain a sense of organizational efficacy and establish a new direction and new sense of control. The message must be: *We control our destiny; It is in our hands*. Anything else is an acknowledgement that chance or the will of others will determine who we are. Operationally, this may require modifying goals, visibly engaging the challenge, or competing in a totally different manner. Imagine a coach telling players at halftime, *"There is nothing we can do. We are beaten"*. Even if it is true, there are other games that will be tainted by that reaction. It is much better to reframe the challenge and say, *"Let's win the second half"*. Many comebacks have been built on that idea. To continue the story of UNC, a group of angry protestors illegally toppled part of the statue on a summer night. This compounded the impression that UNC had lost control and eventually the chancellor was forced out. Before she left, she did have the remaining part of the statue removed, ironically, a hint that she did have authority after all! Organizations can function without control of their destiny, but they are not likely to accomplish very much. Tribes have a strong sense of determination even when the darkest clouds gather. Elections have been won, laws changed, and nations born because determined people believed in their ability to control their destiny.

Commitment

Organizational commitment is the bond or duty a member feels toward their organization. In some sense, it is putting the organizational interests above one's own self-interest. In an ideal situation, self-interest and organizational interest will be the same. A great insight into commitment is offered in the "three component model" developed by John Meyer and Natalie Allen.[7] Affective commitment describes the desire of a member to stay in the organization. If there is positive affective commitment, then a member desires to stay with the organization. They feel valued, satisfied, and are cheerleaders for the organization. Continuance commitment is the need to stay in the organization. If this is positive, then other alternatives are not attractive. The member will not be better off or perhaps they might be worse off if they leave for a different organization. Normative commitment describes the obligation a member feels for remaining with the organization. It is the dissonance one might feel for considering a departure. Perhaps they would disappoint other members by leaving. Or, leaving might adversely increase the workload of fellow members. If normative commitment is high, then there is a strong feeling in members that separation from the organization would create disappointment or hardship. Therefore, there is a strong tendency to remain.

Commitment also manifests itself in the completion of tasks. A committed group of people will do all that is necessary to see a task through to completion. In other words, they do what they say they will do. If for some reason they cannot complete a task or fulfill the obligation, then they will say so. Perhaps the most iconic example of this is the children's story of "The Little Engine that Could."[8] In the story, a long train must be pulled over a high mountain after its engine breaks down. Larger engines are asked to pull the train and for various reasons they refuse. The request is sent to a small engine, who agrees to try. Through determination, optimism, dedication, and commitment, the engine succeeds in pulling the train over the mountain. A modern version of this is captured between Yoda and Luke Skywalker in the Star Wars movie *The Empire Strikes Back*. Yoda asks Luke to use his new-found Jedi skills to raise his star fighter from the swamp. Luke bemoans the task and says, "Alright, I'll give it a try". Yoda responds, "No! Try Not! Do or Do Not! There is no Try!" Both of these examples are endearing testimonies to the power of commitment. It is a bond that seals the efforts of a group to a task and assures members that each is there for the others. Without it, organizations may experience a lot of activity but have very little to show for the effort.

Resolve

Resolve is the determination to act. An organization decides what it should do and then it embarks on the course of action. This should be thought of as a verb rather than a noun. It is action oriented, purposeful, and synonymous with "strength of will". Trust is built on seeing strategy, promises, and plans become actionable marching orders and outcomes. For this to occur, it is sometimes necessary to ignore obstacles and prepare to endure for the long haul. It is the drive that allowed a troubled and nearly deaf musician named Beethoven to compose some of the world's most memorable music. It is the determination that drove a woman named Helen Keller to learn to communicate and also become the first blind person to earn a Bachelor of Arts degree, to read Braille (in English, French, German, Greek, and Latin), and to write and publish numerous books. It is the audacity of Pixar in challenging the assumption that toys could not talk or have feelings when it created *Toy Story*.[9] It is also the ingenuity demonstrated by mission control in the rescue of Apollo 13. In the immortal words of Gene Krantz, the flight control director, "Failure is not an option". Trust is built on the promise and delivery of determined action. Excessive wish making and empty promises create an environment that is anything but innovative. In fact, it is likely to create an environment that is combative and devoid of hope. Yet, in government and in some business organizations, we see copious amounts of hype and less delivery. In essence, these are organizations that dreadfully underperform. Not so in super projects or in very innovative organizations. The difference seems to be how organizations frame the target of their efforts. Innovative entities follow more of a scientific approach in guiding their efforts. They ask questions that can be investigated, they link data to theory, and they develop empirical methods to investigate the question. This reveals a clear path of action that can then be pursed vigorously. In contrast, less innovative entitles spend endless amounts of time half-heartedly chasing multiple paths.[10] Even worse, they stall at the point of action through excessive investigation and debate. For real innovation to occur, resolve must arrive in a timely fashion and must be a visible and definitive call to action.

Consistency

Logic, accuracy, and fairness are the defining traits of organizational consistency. Ideally, an organization reflects its values and beliefs through decisions, rewards, and actions. Consistency removes uncertainty that then results in increased levels of trust. We can count on people to show up, we can see that decisions are made to further objectives, the objectives are aligned with righteous goals, we benefit fairly from our efforts, and all of these things are true day after day. In the realm of commerce, Amazon has built a new empire of business by building predictability and reliability into shipping. Uber and Lyft have risen and fallen based on the levels of consistency in their transportation services.[11] In both instances, customers seek consistency in the services and develop a level or trust and loyalty when those expectations are realized. Within an organization, members seek the same signals and signs of logic from leadership, stakeholders, and each other. A lack of consistency creates an environment in which performance measurement is difficult. It is simply not possible to measure the progress of a journey if the destination is constantly shifting. Messaging (*what* is to be accomplished), structuring activity to take on the task (*how* we will accomplish it), and equity in rewarding the activity (*why* we accomplish it) must be fair and logical to meet the standard of consistency. This leads to trust and efficiency of effort. There is a shared understanding among members, greater coordination, and a better predisposition for change.

Accountability

The final standard of trust is accountability. This can be thought of as the organization's responsibility to its members, the member's responsibility to the organization, and the overall responsibility to the "greater good". Let's start with the greater good. This is rooted in the core belief that an organization should commit itself to humanitarian and social issues and minimize its impact on the environment. While this is commonly thought of as a new and modern principle, it has its genesis in Native American Tribes.[12] These tribes believed that there was a reciprocal relationship between the earth and people. Myths, gods, and ceremonies honored and memorialized aspects of nature and its role in life and living. In today's world a central theme of accountability is positive coexistence between the planet and the organization. The minimal threshold is to do no harm while the ambitious threshold is to improve the world. This is a powerful stimulus and is not necessarily generational. Purpose and legacy are key incentives for motivation and effort for almost everyone.[13] It is part of our DNA. Within the organization, it is important to have systems of accountability that are based on driving improvement, have two-way avenues of feedback, and have established lines of ownership between responsibilities and those expected to accomplish them. There is a great story in baseball that highlights accountability and how easy it is to misattribute and misshape it. The great baseball manager and Hall of Famer Frankie Frisch asked a rookie to play center field. The rookie promptly dropped the first fly ball that was hit to him. On the next play he let a grounder go between his feet and then threw the ball to the wrong base. Frankie stormed out of the dugout, took the glove away from the rookie, and said, "I'll show you how to play this position". The next batter slammed a line drive right over second base. Frankie ran in on it, missed it completely, fell down when he tried to chase it, threw down his glove, and yelled at the rookie, "You've got center field so screwed up nobody can play it". The moral of the story: sometimes the most difficult aspect of accountability is holding ourselves accountable.

The Manifestation of Trust: Knowledge and Knowledge Flows

Another important aspect of trust is its manifestation in the creation and flow of knowledge throughout the organization. The standards speak to the cultural aspect of trust. Knowledge and knowledge flows are trust captured in action. The two go hand in hand and together provide a means to assess how well an organization is positioned to capture, convert, and apply what it knows and what it learns. It is useful to look at this from two perspectives: First, the capability of an organization to create knowledge and second the flow of knowledge throughout the organization.

Knowledge Capability

A key to understanding the success and failure of knowledge management within organizations is identification and assessment of preconditions that are necessary for the effort to flourish. Of course, strong standards of trust must be in place to set a cultural context. However, other preconditions that address knowledge capability must also be in place. Organizations must develop an "absorptive capacity"—the ability to use prior knowledge to recognize the value of new information, assimilate it, and apply it to create new knowledge.[14] Therefore, beyond the standards of trust, organizations must develop capability to learn, archive what is learned, and combine what is learned with what is archived to create new knowledge. Then, there must be an efficient marketplace of knowledge within the organization. As shown in Figure 5.2, a useful way to frame knowledge capability is to separate it into two components[15]:

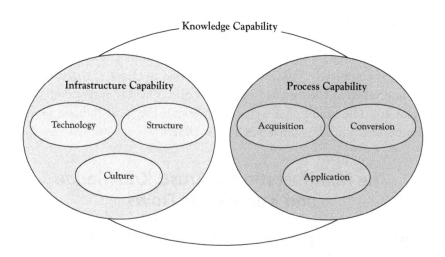

Figure 5.2: Trust and Knowledge Capability

1. *Infrastructure Capabilities:* The basic foundational characteristics of an organization needed for creating and exchanging knowledge.
2. *Process Capabilities:* The combination of methods and people used in creating and exchanging knowledge.

Infrastructure Capabilities

Technology comprises a crucial element of capability needed to capture, archive, and create new knowledge. Through the linkage of information and communication systems in an organization, previously fragmented flows of information and knowledge can be integrated. These linkages can also eliminate barriers to communication that naturally occur between different parts of the organization. Since technology is multifaceted, the organization must invest in a comprehensive infrastructure that supports the various types of knowledge and communication that are critical. It is very tempting to think of this capability as something new and modern. Far from the truth! Drawings in caves, on parchment, and on animal pelts were technologies used by ancient tribes to capture and share knowledge. Dance, song, stories, and ceremonies were also used for the same purpose. Signal stations, lighthouses, and Morse code are also clever ways to transfer knowledge. The point is that it is important to think broadly about technology. It is a means of capture and a means of flow. This can be done through a conversation or a sophisticated system of digital technology. Applying the right amount and combination of high-tech and high-touch is the magic in establishing the technological capability. The answers to key questions should not live in e-mails, texts, complex digital archives, or tweets. There needs to be a technological infrastructure that brings the answers off the backroads on to the organizational interstate.

Organizational structure is important in leveraging technological architecture. While structure is intended to rationalize individual functions or units within an organization, structural elements have often had the unintended consequence of inhibiting collaboration and sharing of knowledge across internal organizational boundaries. For example, structures that promote individualistic behavior in which locations, divisions, and functions are rewarded for 'hoarding' information can inhibit effective knowledge management across the organization. If the same people have all the answers all the time, if every report or project seems like it begins from scratch, and if critical knowledge disappears when a member leaves, then there may be a structural problem. In the classic scene from the movie *The Pink Panther Strikes Again,*

Inspector Clouseau enters an Inn. He sees a dog resting in the lobby and asks the innkeeper, "*Does your dog bite?*" The innkeeper replies, "*No*". The inspector reaches to pet the dog. The dog ferociously bites him on the hand. The Inspector yells at the innkeeper, "*I thought you said your dog did not bite!*" The Innkeeper replies, "*That is not my dog*". Good structure should not only ensure accuracy of knowledge, it should also facilitate understanding.

Along with standards of trust and structure, culture plays an important part in building capability. Interaction between individuals is essential in the innovation process. Dialogue between individuals or groups are often the basis for the creation of new ideas and can therefore be viewed as having the potential for creating knowledge. Employee interaction should be encouraged, both formally and informally, so that relationships, contacts, and perspectives are shared by those not working side by side. This type of interaction and collaboration is important when attempting to transmit tacit knowledge between individuals or convert tacit knowledge into explicit knowledge, thereby transforming it from individual to organizational level. In addition, employees should have the ability to self-organize their own networks of knowledge and practice to facilitate solutions to new or existing problems and to generate or share knowledge. Sometimes, the culture we make can kill innovation and knowledge transfer although we set up the culture in hopes of achieving the opposite. I remember attending an MBA graduation. I was the faculty member who was assigned the role of hosting our graduation speaker, Michael Armstrong, CEO of AT&T. I stood on the stage with Mr. Armstrong and our dean as the graduates filed into the auditorium. Mr. Armstrong commented on how distinguished our graduates looked. He then asked our dean if they were innovative. Without hesitation, our dean said, "*Well, they were when they arrived here!*" This bit of self-deprecating humor had an important message. We all hoped that the MBA experience had not harmed or taken away their natural urge to be creative and to dream. Graduate business study is not designed to do so, but one can't help but wonder.

Process Capabilities

Part of managing knowledge and creating trust within the organization is developing processes that acquire knowledge. Two primary means of collecting knowledge are (1) to seek and acquire entirely new knowledge or (2) create new knowledge out of existing knowledge through collaboration between individuals and between organizations. This is an important part of a truly tribal approach. Individuals, groups of individuals, and organizations (or tribes) actively create knowledge for a shared purpose. This is something very identifiable in super projects such as Event Horizon Telescope, Lawrence Berkeley Lab, New Horizons, and OpenAI. The network of collaboration is robust and extremely cooperative. Particularly along the dimension of knowledge creation and transfer. Acquiring knowledge is costly and time consuming. It must be identified, shaped into a useful form, and then authenticated. Sharing this process across tribes builds efficiency and pockets of unique specialization. Knowing where the wellsprings of knowledge are within a tribal network and how to access them is to create extra knowledge capacity. The wheel is not reinvented every time there is an identified need for knowledge or expertise. Knowledge is only created when it is not part of the tribal network.

An organization must also acquire the ability to make knowledge useful (i.e., convert it into a useful form). This process characteristic is conversion. The organization must organize and structure knowledge, thereby making it easier to access and distribute it within the organization. By combining or integrating knowledge, redundancy can be reduced, and efficiency can be improved by reducing excess volume. As developed by Nonaka and Takeuchi,[16] organizational knowledge starts at the individual level with thoughts or understanding. It then evolves as individuals' dialogue with their colleagues. The ideas are then articulated and converted to a form that can be widespread. As described, tacit knowledge, which is difficult to codify, evolves to some form of explicit knowledge which is easier to codify, as it diffuses throughout an organization. Conversion is a key process in taking what is known in concept and experience in individuals and making it accessible to the organization. In super projects, this is done through complex data visualization and presentations based on simulations, animation, and virtual reality. The noticeable aspect of this conversion is the interactivity and engagement that it encompasses. If a picture is worth a thousand words, becoming immersed in the picture and able to engage in its context is worth a thousand pictures!

Knowledge application processes are oriented toward the use of knowledge. This is more difficult than one might initially guess. We now live in a world of information. You might say we are in an age of exaggeration. Information and knowledge are bigger and more dramatic viewed through the lens of modern media and technology. The first step in navigating this landscape is to clearly separate what is known from what is not known and to accept that a great amount of knowledge is debatable. It is easy to develop a sense that knowledge is a dichotomy of what is known or what is not known. If something is not known, then we investigate it and then it becomes known. If only it were that easy! In science, politics, business, or religion there is knowledge that is debatable. Before we apply knowledge, we must know its true state. Only then can it lead to good decisions. We must also know ourselves, and we must not forget the important role wisdom plays in knowledge application. Research has shown that the *less* of an expert someone is in a field, the more they tend to overestimate their ability. Plus, there is a strong tendency in these same people to be a poor judge of the skills of others. Further, those that are *most* skilled tend to underestimate their abilities.[17] If you want to see an example of this, then just browse the comments section of any online news article or watch a panel of "experts" on any news channel. Therefore, there is a very steep human bias to overcome in applying knowledge successfully. Not all knowledge is understanding, and there is a strong tendency to incorrectly estimate our ability to use it, expert or non-expert. Knowing the true nature of knowledge and our potential reaction to it is important to create effective application processes. In ancient tribes, wisdom filled in these important gaps. An outside set of eyes, someone who has no emotional stake in the decision, or someone who has been there before can be an important wellspring of wisdom. As stated in an Arapahoe proverb, *"If we wonder often then knowledge will come"*.

The Flow of Knowledge

Along with capability, an organization must create a robust, consistent, and predictable flow of knowledge. This flow should be both "pull" and "push". Members should be able to easily seek, identify, and "pull" the knowledge they need from the organization. They should also be able to receive knowledge "push" from the organization about new science, events, or environmental changes that may impact their work. As illustrated in Figure 5.3, there are four major types of knowledge flow. These flows are from member to member, tribe to member, member to tribe, and tribe to tribe. Each plays a critical role in building trust and coordination within and between tribes. This perspective is useful in determining where knowledge roadblocks occur and where there are clear highways of knowledge flow. Ideally, there are robust flows across these four domains. If this is true, and knowledge capabilities are intact, then the probability of bigger and better ideas is very high.

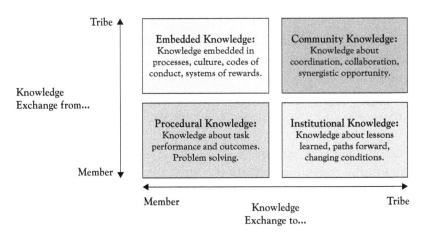

Figure 5.3: Flows of Knowledge in and between Tribes

Procedural knowledge flows from member to member. This knowledge content is based on "know-how" about how to accomplish task, how to assess outcomes, and how to solve problems. It is a critical flow that cannot be encumbered by incentives or prior experiences that motivate members to stop sharing "what they know". The instincts of emergent structure as well as roles combine with the instinct of trust to create a context for rich knowledge flows between members. This flow is based in fact, is demonstrable, and is directly applicable. Knowledge that does not meet these standards is discouraged and often deemed more of a hazard than a help.

Embedded knowledge flows from the tribe to the member. This is knowledge content that conveys culture, process, codes of conduct, and systems of rewards. It aligns closely with the instincts of ambition and emergent structure to keep members focused and rewarded. In traditional settings, this flow is too often ignored or heavily codified in strategy documents and other policy/procedure. In addition, the flow might only occur sporadically, at the beginning of a project, or when a crisis hits. In the groups of this study, this flow, along with institutional knowledge (discussed next), is a constant stream of guiding principles, adjustments, and contingencies that create quick adaptability.

Institutional knowledge flows from the member to the tribe. Again, emergent structure and roles help to make this a robust flow. One role in particular seems crucial in developing institutional knowledge. The role of *seeker* formally assigns the activity of gathering and exchanging knowledge from within the tribe and between tribes to a member. This is a powerful mechanism when teams of people are working on various aspects of a shared project. It is also powerful when teams are not working on shared projects. This is because projects, however diverse, will have common problem sets and coping strategies. Bringing to the tribe lessons learned, promising paths forward, and the collective knowledge that exists outside the tribe creates velocity in moving forward, eliminates duplicity, and takes better advantage of available resources.

Finally, *community knowledge* is rooted in collaboration, cooperation, and synergistic opportunities between tribes. Again, the formal role of a seeker within each tribe can facilitate this exchange. Another tactic that has great effect is cross assignment of members between tribes. The concept of a "tribal council" is also a noticeable coordinating structure in this flow. Leaders of tribes (architects) meet not only to provide updates on their progress, they also share stories about their tribes' challenges, victories, and journey. In these councils, ceremony and storytelling become important avenues of creating rich flows of community knowledge. Like knowledge, other flows of resources (time, money, technology) move openly and fairly between tribes and members when the tribal instinct of trust is present. These flows, along with honest communication and stories about what is prized, what is feared, and what might be done, are key aspects of building the instinct of trust.[18]

Trust is a very interesting concept, and this chapter has framed it in a bit of a different way. Given that a tribal effort is something bigger, more meaningful, and more personal to members, there is a deeper and more cerebral aspect of trust. This is captured in the standards of trust. This can be thought of as the socialization aspect of the concept. Values, norms, and codes of conduct are applicable and address relationships between members and between members and the organization. However, there is also an operational aspect of trust. This addresses how the organization acquires, converts, and distributes knowledge. This marketplace in terms of capabilities and flow can create a fluid, coordinated, and adaptable organization. Standards and capabilities work hand-in-hand to build trust. If you are a leader or a contributor, it is important to constantly assess the state of trust within the organization. The structure described here is an obvious ally in the efforts of today's most innovative projects. It is also something that has guided innovative groups of people through their toughest times. Championship teams, iconic bands, and everyday people accomplish the extraordinary when bound by trust.

Notes

1. Tom Harrison, *Living Through The Blitz*. London: Faber & Faber, 2010.
2. Albert H. Segars, "Effective Communication of Corporate Crisis Through the Internet," *Business Strategy Review*, 14(3), Autumn 2003.
3. Albert H. Segars and Gary F. Kohut, "Strategic Communication Through the World Wide Web: An Empirical Model of Effectiveness in CEO's Letter to Shareholders," *Journal of Management Studies*, 38(4), June 2001.
4. Robert M. Galford and Anne Seibold Drapeau, "The Enemies of Trust," *Harvard Business Review*, February 2003.
5. Robert B. Cialdini, Petia K. Petrova and Noah Goldstein, "The Hidden Costs of Organizational Dishonesty," *Sloan Management Review*, Spring 2004.
6. Valerie Bauerlein, "UNC Chancellor to Step Down Amid Silent Sam Rift," *Wall Street Journal*, July 15, 2019.
7. John P. Meyer and Natalie Allen, "A Three Component Conceptualization of Organizational Commitment," *Human Resource Management Review*, 1(1), Spring 1991.
8. Rev. Charles S. Wing, "Story of the Engine That Thought it Could," *New York Tribune*, April 8, 1906.
9. Walter Isaacson, "The Real Leadership Lessons of Steve Jobs," *Harvard Business Review*, April 2012.
10. Jack Zenger and Joseph Folkman, "The 3 Elements of Trust," *Harvard Business Review*, February 2019.
11. Greg Benslinger, "Uber Posts Slower Sales Gains, Widening Loss as It Prepares for 2019 IPO," *Wall Street Journal*, July 16, 2019.
12. Annie L. Booth, "We are the Land: Native American Views of Nature," *Nature Across Cultures*, Kluwer Academic Publishers, pp. 329–349, 2003.
13. Daniel H. Pink, *Drive: The Surprising Truth About What Motivates Us*. Riverhead Books, 2009.
14. W. Cohen and D. Levinthal, "Absorptive Capacity: A New Perspective on Learning and Innovation." *Administrative Science Quarterly*, 35, 128–152, 1990.
15. A. Gold, A. Malhotra, and A. Segars. "Knowledge Management: An Organizational Capabilities Perspective," *Journal of Management Information Systems*, 18, 185–214, 2001.
16. Ikujior Nonaka and Hirotaka Takeuchi, *The Knowledge-Creating Company: How Japanese Companies Create the Dynamics of Innovation*. Oxford University Press, 1995.
17. Justin Kruger and David Dunning, "Unskilled and Unaware of It: How Difficulties in Recognizing One's Own Incompetence Lead to Inflated Self-Assessments," *Journal of Personality and Social Psychology*, 77(6), 1999.
18. Liz Ryan, "Ten Ways to Build Trust on your Teams," *Forbes*, March 17, 2018.

· 6 ·

NAVIGATION

Numbers have life; they're not just symbols on paper.

— Shakuntala Devi

As suggested by the insightful quote of Shakuntala Devi, numbers have life. They tell stories and they take us places. They have taken people to the moon, they have helped us navigate the seas, and they tell us when things are going well and when they are not going so well. As a tribal instinct, the ability to capture, formulate, and interpret numbers is *navigation*. There are three important aspects of this activity: (1) *linking* and aligning numbers, analytics, and performance indicators, (2) *causal* interpretation of the linkages, and (3) *determination* if the linkages are moving the tribe toward the intended outcome. Tribes are well equipped for this activity because of their deep appreciation for stories (interpretation) and knowledge (numbers and context). Plus, the trait of resourcefulness places emphasis on gathering only the signs, data points, or stories that are most relevant while leaving unneeded information behind. Tribal navigation is rooted in the ability to identify systems of numbers and relationships that link the efforts of the tribe to success measures and then to the intended objective. It can be thought of as choosing the compass that not only signals direction, but also signals how well you are progressing toward the objective. I conceptualize the activity of navigation as a "chain of logic". This chain links the initiatives of the tribe with intended objectives. As developed, it is a system that may be viewed differently in theory and in numbers, its logic may shift over time, and organizations may or may not reconnoiter these chains as conditions change. Recalibrating a chain of logic is not easy. As I saw on a bumper sticker one day, "Change is good, you go first!" Yet, to be tribal is know when shifts occur and how they impact the organizational chain of logic. Let's develop these concepts in more detail.

Chains of Logic

Organizations and individuals build chains of logic for a number of endeavors. For example, an outcome of professional success might be linked with initiatives of performing well in k-12, scoring well on college admission tests, gaining admission to a great university, achieving an undergraduate degree, and maybe getting a Masters of Business Administration. Along the way you gather and generate data such as grades, rankings, and other endorsements. That data then becomes a system of analytics that are patterns of statistics and insights. Some of these analytics and other knowledge become key performance indicators. As long as that chain is valid, then you can accurately calibrate your initiatives with your intended outcome. More so, you can measure your progress against others seeking similar outcomes. Universities should also observe this chain and align their chain of logic accordingly. This is important: chains of logic live within codependent ecosystems. As long as there is harmony, then all is understood and all is predictable. This is illustrated in Figure 6.1.

To be fair, I have taken a very general view in describing and illustrating a chain of logic. The amount and sophistication of psychology and the amount and sophistication of numbers are far greater than those depicted. When interactions between numbers and psychology are added, the equation gets very complex. However, the key point to remember is that individuals and organizations develop targeted outcomes. To achieve the outcome, they create and launch a set of initiatives. They then set up a system of measurement to calibrate what they do (initiatives) with what they want to achieve (outcomes). How this is done is sometimes the work of genius and sometimes not so much. A story will illustrate the point.

In 2012, the National Football League experienced a labor dispute with the NFL Referees Association. This resulted in a "lockout" of regular referees.

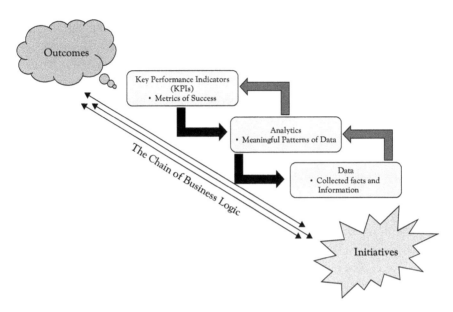

Figure 6.1: A Chain of Logic

In their place, "replacement" referees were used to officiate the first three weeks of the NFL season. As the replacement officials began missing calls, a powerful chain of logic began to take shape. If the owners would settle with the union, then the regular officials could return to the field and the excessive missed calls would stop. The outcome, better officiating, would be realized if the owners seized the imitative to settle with the union. The performance part of the chain is simply correct play calling. I became intrigued and wondered if the chain and its interpretation were valid. The logic seemed to indicate that the chain was intact and predictable until replacement officials were introduced. It was not difficult to get data on NFL officiating. Granted, it was not perfect data, but it was possible to see definitive trends in officiating (1970 until 2012) and if the change in officials resulted in a dramatic increase in bad calls. The results were very telling. Officiating had steadily become worse over the years. In addition, the number of questionable calls by replacement officials was not statistically different from what would have been expected from regular officials.[1] Why? My guess is that the game has become more sophisticated over the years. Players are now super athletes. Coaches are very sophisticated in creating offensive and defensive schemes. Plus, rules have become more plentiful and difficult to apply. Basically, the sophistication of the game has made it very difficult to officiate. Yes, the replacement officials may have had a higher predisposition to miss a call but the storm of news coverage that demonized them missed the underlying problem that still haunts the game. The NFL owners settled the lockout but the bad officiating continues.[2]

Setting a valid chain of logic begins with defining the right outcome. As noted in the chapter on ambition, it is tempting to define an outcome that is too localized and too small. For example, it was not Apple's intention to build a device in the ipod project. Instead, the outcome was to revolutionize the experience of listening to music.[3] Through discovery, this experience manifested itself in the capability to listen to anything you wanted wherever you wanted. Ten thousand songs at your fingertip, wherever you might be. Once you have the right outcome, then initiatives and objectives are easier to put into place. The logic of the chain starts to build and come into focus. Finally, systems of measurement tell you if the progress is efficient and if you are on course. This sequence is very important. Too many times, organizations will start with initiatives, set systems of measurement, and then acquire the target. Ironically, this sometimes works. However, it is not a viable strategy for innovation. Although it is tempting to declare victory once you develop a perfectly aligned chain of logic, the race is not fully won. The final lap in the mile is to build adaptability into the chain. Sometimes the best outcome will shift, the recipe of initiatives that achieved an outcome no longer works, or the system of measurement is no longer reliable. Similar to the emergence of super athletes, sophisticated coaches, and complex rules in the NFL, a fundamental shift occurs. This may lead to a need to reconfigure a chain of logic.

Shifting Outcomes

The theory of disruptive innovation provides a great perspective for understanding dramatic shifts in outcomes.[4] The basic idea is that established organizations can lose their place to unexpected competitors. Borrowing from these ideas, let's shift the focus away from new competitors to outcomes. In any organizational situation, there is the possibility that a perfectly aligned chain of logic can be shaken by a shift in outcome. This shift can be due to technology, preferences, or newly discovered ways of working. This is illustrated in Figure 6.2.

The story begins in a very positive way. An incumbent organization has identified an outcome that is ambitious and has launched a set of initiatives

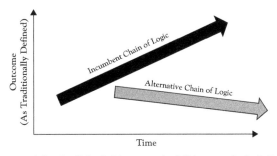

An Incumbent Chain og Logic improves over time, Initiatives appear to be aligned with outcomes and systems of measurement. Alternative Chains of Logic that have different sets of alignment and chase different outcomes appear inferior and foolish.

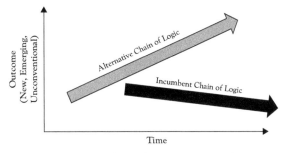

The Alternative Chain of Logic matches an emerging, important, and new outcome. This chain improves over time against the new outcome. The Incumbent Chain of Logic is an ill fit for the new outcome. The more it is fortified the worse it performs against the new outcome.

Figure 6.2: Shifting Outcomes and Chains of Logic

that enable it to achieve the outcome. Systems of measurement are accurate and reliable. As the organization achieves more success and perfects the chain of logic, the outcome becomes almost mythical. It is impossible to imagine other outcomes and other chains. Yet, on the radar screen appears an alternative chain of logic. The alternative sequence operates in the incumbent's sphere of influence but seems nonsensical. It may hit a different outcome with a very different alignment of initiatives and measurement systems. Think of a soda such as Coca Cola as the incumbent and a bottle of water as the alternative. In this case, sugar, caffeine, and formula are the targeted outcome of Coke. Water seems strangely inadequate and nonsensical when measured against this outcome. The magic is that water is hitting a new, emerging, and important alternative outcome. That outcome is hydration. When we replace the incumbent outcome of sugar, caffeine, and formula with the alternative outcome of hydration, then the alternative chain of logic dominates the incumbent chain. This represents a fundamental shift in logic or disruption.

The ability to sense these dynamics and adapt accordingly is part of the tribal perspective. These shifts can occur in almost any aspect of commerce, medicine, or life. The key is to keep an eye on outcomes and not technology, media, talking heads, or other embodiments or vehicles of outcome. The critical question is: What is the fundamental outcome that drives this organization and is it important?

Three Deadly Responses

As illustrated in Figure 6.3, when a significant shift in outcome occurs, it becomes necessary to recast the chain of logic. The theory of disruptive innovation suggests that chains are more easily invented than adjusted. Therefore, it will be the new, entrepreneurial organization that sees the new outcome and orchestrates the chain of logic to meet it. However, it is also possible that organizations assemble a chain of logic for an outcome that quickly disappears or shifts again. Clearly, spotting a shifting outcome is tough and, yes, maybe even tougher for established organizations. My research suggests that such organizations have lost their tribal instinct. They will resist moving to a new

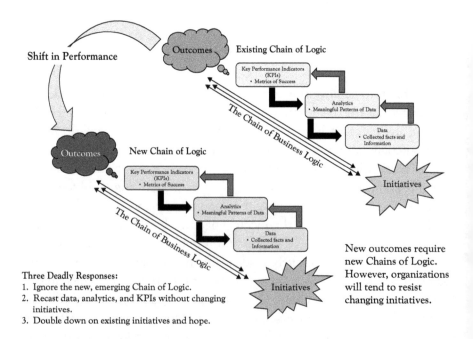

Figure 6.3: Shifting Models of Logic

chain of logic and do almost anything to stay the course. For these organizations, three deadly responses are likely.

The first deadly response is to ignore and maybe ridicule the new chain of logic. Leadership might even go so far as to say that organizations, customers, and employees love us so much that chasing a new outcome would be more dangerous than staying the course. I call this the "Sears Mistake". Sears was a powerhouse of U.S. retail for many years. The symbol of their prominence was the "Sears Tower" in Chicago. However, changing demographics, styles, and the emergence of online retail created an outcome that Sears was unwilling to chase. Leadership was not blind to these changes. They just underestimated the magnitude and direction of the shift. Plus, to be fair, they were encouraged to keep their chain of logic by employees, suppliers, and industry experts. The signs were in clear sight; the instinct of navigation was not in place.

The second deadly response is to recast the data analytics and performance indicators so that they tell you things are great. The initiatives and the outcome of the chain remain fixed. I call this the "Nortel Mistake". Nortel was a world leader in telecommunication technology. However, when the network revolution took shape, voice and data converged into digital signals and new network technology dominated the marketplace. The leader of the new revolution was Cisco. Rather than adopt the new logic, Nortel recast its compass such that their way of doing business still seemed solid. In essence, the organization changed the schemes of measurement to make alignment of initiatives and outcome seem logical. The problem was that the financial markets did not believe the rationale and Nortel lost all of its market value. Again, leadership was not blind. There was no surprise. The company lost its sense of navigation and more importantly its ability to adapt.

A third deadly response is to believe that more throttle on the existing chain will produce results. I call this the "Xerox Mistake". I saw this mistake firsthand when working with Xerox as a consultant. Xerox was losing share in copiers and printers. Cloud networks, adobe acrobat, and digital storage were shifting the outcome of document management. Instead of competing against this landscape, the company doubled down on pushing its sales force. This tactic had no effect. Even the best salespeople could not sell into that marketplace. Customers did not want the equipment. They were looking for digital and software solutions. This response is more prominent that one might believe at first glance. As I experienced, to point this out to a hard charging leader is not easy and brings a very swift rebuke. Whipping a dead horse is no recipe for running faster.

An organization with a tribal mentality will avoid these mistakes. Adaptation is part of the fabric woven into all aspects of the chain of logic. Even in the best of times, there is an undercurrent of belief that nothing lasts forever. In fact, this belief is a foundation for finding new and exciting sources of opportunity. This was very visible in the super projects I researched. Evolving science, new ways of exchanging data, and the creation of knowledge were seen as something very necessary to evolve and adapt chains of logic. This was not something to be feared. It was something expected, welcomed, and shaped. It is the adjustment made at halftime when the game plan is not working. The search for a new job when the one you have is not meeting your financial or career aspirations. The request for a second opinion to make sure you get the medical care you need. It is an important instinct. So, how do we see the new outcome? The obvious answer is in the data, analytics, and performance indicators. They should signal trouble if we believe them. However, there is something more than numbers that makes the task tough. There is theory. This is the belief about the chain of logic that is based on experience and sometimes outright opinion. The comingling of numbers and theory is complex and can often lead to strange decisions. Let's take a look.

Conventional Wisdom and Numbers

One of the most interesting aspects of navigation is the marriage of *conventional wisdom* (expert opinion, accepted practice, commentary) with *numbers* (data, metrics).[5] Every chain of logic will have numbers that attest to its effectiveness and relevance. These can be measures of voter approval, growth in market share, winning percentage, etc., in essence, any quantifiable measure of performance. There is also conventional wisdom. This is the opinion, view of the world, or perspective of experts, academics, and leaders in the field. It can also be a stream of belief that runs through an organization. It is not entirely based on fact and sometimes involves a lot of extrapolating from the past and a lot of speculation about the future. It can also emerge over time without formal validation. There is nothing wrong with conventional wisdom as long as it is recognized as such. It is fascinating and it is many times that part of knowledge that is debatable. However, it is also powerful and something that can be shaped to create a context of poor decision making. Together, numbers and conventional wisdom frame the perception of effectiveness for a chain of logic. However, there is a paradox. Conventional wisdom does not always align with numbers. Experts may praise and endorse a chain of logic that does not perform well in numbers, and vice versa. Further, conventional wisdom will tend to trail numbers in yielding an accurate assessment. In other words, the chain of logic will show promise or problems in numbers before it shows promise or problems in conventional wisdom. This can create uncertainty in assessing the validity of the chain. To help shape this frontier, I have framed these possibilities as a matrix of conventional wisdom, numbers, and logic. It is presented in Figure 6.4. Using this tool, it is possible to get a better sense of what is working and what is failing in conventional wisdom and numbers. The instinct of navigation is rooted in understanding the potential alignment and disconnect between these two frames of effectiveness.

When wisdom and numbers indicate that a chain of logic is successful, "*Sound Logic*" prevails. As illustrated, I call this frontier the "*Yellow Brick Road*". This space represents the current "state of the art". Professors in MBA classrooms will praise these businesses, and the stock market also rewards them with strong valuation. Certain political campaigns will be lauded by the political pundits and those candidates will win elections. Professional sports teams follow chains of logic in acquiring players, coaches, and developing ways of playing that are heralded by sportswriters; and those teams win championships. In short, there is a strong alignment between the experts and the

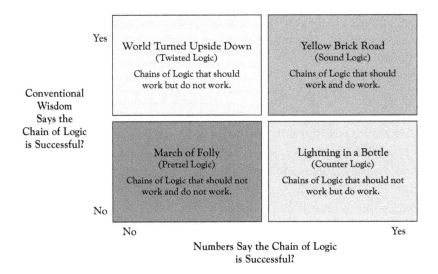

Figure 6.4: Conventional Wisdom, Numbers, and Logic

realized numbers. This does not mean it will last forever. However, in the present environment, these chains of logic are sound and solid.

At the other extreme, chains of logic in which wisdom and numbers indicate a lack of success are called a *March of Folly*. Although it seems illogical, some wayward organizations still attempt to implement these chains. The reason for this is *Pretzel Logic*: a system of logic that supports a nonsensical conclusion, primarily, a belief that the outcome will be somehow different for the perpetrator because of special insights or capabilities. This is very seldom true. As mentioned earlier, Custer's last stand against the Lakota Nation is a vivid example of this logic. The U.S. housing bubble of 2008 and subsequent recession is another great example. This crisis was caused by the inability of a large number of homeowners to pay their mortgages as their low introductory-rate mortgages reverted to regular interest rates. Risky lending, easy money, and fraud were known to be trouble; the numbers backed it up but the train kept rolling until the bubble burst.[6] Even very innovative organizations can make this mistake. Apple's attempt to add music by the rock band U2 to the iTunes account of all their customers without their customers' consent is a shining example.[7] Whenever you hear the phrases "*it will be different for us*" or "*they did not know what we know*" or "*the world has changed since then*", be aware. A March of Folly might lie ahead.

When wisdom signals success but the numbers signal trouble, the result is a "*World Turned Upside Down*". Again, some organizations will attempt this chain believing the numbers are not as strong of a signal as wisdom. In this context, *twisted logic* prevails. Everything that once worked for an organization begins to work against it or "*all you know is wrong*". The typical origin of this situation is the belief that a yellow brick road chain is transferable to any context. The use of World War II fighting tactics in the jungles of Vietnam was a very stark example of this logic for the United States Military. Wal Mart's unsuccessful entry into Germany and other European countries is an example of this twisted logic in today's context of business. In politics, the presidential campaign of Hillary Clinton might be considered the use of political tactics and a chain of logic that was heralded in prevailing theory (it worked for her husband, Bill Clinton, in the 1990s), but it was a surprising failure in numbers.[8] The song "A World Turned Upside Down" was played by the musicians of the British army as they surrendered to Washington at Yorktown. If you hear the phrases "*it worked then so it will work now*", "*it works here so it will work there*", or "this should work", you may be embarking upon the strange frontier of the upside down.

The most interesting context of shifting chains of logic is *"Lightning in a Bottle"*. *Counter logic* prevails in this situation because wisdom suggests failure while numbers signal success. This is the context of the most innovative organizations. This is also where the decoupling of theory and numbers is most important. As Wilber and Orville Wright experimented with their flying machines at the turn of the century, many leading experts ridiculed and scoffed at their efforts. Yet, their experiments yielded data and results that defied much of the prevailing conventional wisdom. Although they were two brothers from nowhere, bicycle makers, and not part of the intellectual elite, they demonstrated every aspect of tribal instinct in their process of invention. Particularly, a mastery of logic that matched their initiatives to outcomes.[9] Something as simple as a bottle of water or as grandiose as a web site that allows you to purchase anything you want from anywhere you might be is a powerful reminder that "lightening in the bottle" types of initiatives can completely recast prevailing chains of logic. From running a four-minute mile to the exploration of Pluto, many great feats are built on belief in the numbers and the audacity to challenge conventional wisdom.[10]

In this chapter we have viewed the instinct of navigation from the perspective of logic. Organizations set up chains of initiatives, systems of measurement, and targeted outcomes as a means of rationalizing their existence. When these chains are in harmony, the organization is on the right course and it can have confidence that any adjustments that need to be made will be signaled and quickly implemented. To be tribal is to seek the right outcome, choose initiatives that are logically consistent with achieving the outcome, and create a compass that keeps the tribe on course. It is also the ability to adapt new chains when they are needed, abandon chains when they are failing, or modify a chain that is struggling. This ability to adapt may be the toughest to acquire and live with. Wisdom and numbers interact in strange ways to confound the building of good logic. Yet, there is a huge opportunity for those organizations that realistically assess current logic and can envision the prevailing logic that will be needed in the coming waves of technological, scientific, and business innovation.

Notes

1. Kevin Clark, "The NFL Replacement Ref Audit," *Wall Street Journal*, September 19, 2012.
2. Jason Gay, "Is this a Stolen Super Bowl? Well ….," *Wall Street Journal*, January 27, 2019.
3. Leander Kahney, *The Cult of iPod*. No Starch Press, 2005.

4. Clayton Christenson, *The Innovators, Dilemma: When New Technologies Cause Great Firms to Fail*, Harvard Business Review Press, 2015.
5. Joan Magretta, "Why Business Models Matter," *Harvard Business Review*, 80(5), June 2002.
6. Alan Greenspan, "The Roots of the Mortgage Crisis," *Wall Street Journal*, December 12, 2007.
7. Erik Sherman, "Apple's $100 Million U2 Debacle," *CBS News*, September 17, 2014.
8. Pete Stevenson, Trump Is Headed for a Win, Says Professor Who Has Predicted 30 Years of Presidential Outcomes Correctly, *The Washington Post*, September 23, 2016.
9. David McCullough, *The Wright Brothers*. Simon and Schuster, 2015.
10. Bill Taylor, "What the Four Minute Mile Taught Us About the Limits of Conventional Thinking," *Harvard Business Review*, March 2018.

· 7 ·

PERSEVERANCE

We fight, get beat, rise, and fight again.
— General Nathanael Greene, United States Continental Army, 1778

I grew up in a small town, Camden, South Carolina. It was a great place to grow up and it is still a place I love to visit. Although it is not widely known, an incredible event that helped Americans achieve their independence took place about six miles north of the town in August 1780. It is known as the Battle of Camden. A significant force of the Continental army and militia led by General Horatio Gates met the well-trained British force led by Lord Cornwallis. It was a miserable defeat for the Continentals. Many tactical mistakes were made and the grand army simply disintegrated. General Gates abandoned the field and rode horseback seventy miles without stopping. Whether the ride of Gates was fear, cowardice, or good horsemanship is still under debate by the historians. So why was this so important? Because after the debacle, General George Washington named Nathanael Greene commanding general of the southern forces. Greene was a master of tactics, a detailed planner, and a realist. Unlike Gates, Greene knew that the key to eventual victory was not to win grand battles, it was to endure. This was particularly true because the British were operating far from home in a very inhospitable part of the world. Practicing unconventional warfare, Greene harassed the

British, yet lost several battles. However, in doing so, he weakened the British army. Lord Cornwallis said of Greene, "No General has gained more by losing battles!" The endurance and tactics of Greene's forces pushed Cornwallis out of the Carolinas. This eventually led to the capture of Cornwallis' army at Yorktown. Greene's mindset was tribal and the instinct in action was that of perseverance.

Dimensions of Perseverance

As shown if Figure 7.1, perseverance is built on three interrelated principles: persistence, endurance, and patience. This is the part of innovation that is almost never discussed. It does not fit the attractive narrative of quick ideas and instant success. The reality is that ideas are elusive. Ideas hide in the noise and distraction of everyday life. They are threatening and they may challenge assumptions. In their early forms, ideas are more like ugly ducklings than beautiful swans. Unlike conventional paths, innovative paths are full of winding turns and unexpected detours. Victory is not easy. It is something that is hard-won. All of this speaks to the attribute of *persistence*. Continuing forward in the face of difficulty is tough for any organization or individual. It is easy to lose faith, to turn back, or to simply give up. The untold story of innovation is that there will be setbacks. The best way to deal with them is to acknowledge that they will happen before the march is begun. If the organization has no tolerance for pain, then it is better to be average. In the most innovative organizations, setbacks are not only expected, they are welcomed. Hardship is a chance to demonstrate the full capability of the organization and make

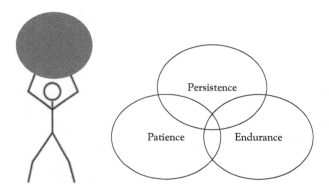

Figure 7.1: Dimensions of Perseverance

it stronger. Stories of persistence are very inspiring. African-American track star, Wilma Rudolph, suffered scarlet fever, whooping cough, and measles, survived infantile paralysis, and required a leg brace until age nine. She went on to win three Olympic gold medals and was considered the "Fastest woman on Earth". J.K. Rowling became the world's best-selling children's author, despite living on governmental benefits as a single mother. Initially, her manuscript for *Harry Potter* was rejected by several publishers.

Endurance is the ability to not "break" under pressure. It speaks to the strength and grit of an organization or individual as they face hardship. It also speaks to the "grace" or "style" in which the hardship is handled. Here is an example. Even today, with advanced foods, radios, and insulated clothing, a journey on foot across Antarctica is one of the harshest tests a human being can be asked to endure. A hundred years ago, it was far worse. Then, wool clothing absorbed snow and damp. High-energy food came in an unappetizing mix of rendered fats called pemmican. Worst of all, extremes of cold pervaded everything. During a scientific expedition in the Antarctic in 1912–13, Douglas Mawson lost his colleagues 300 miles from safety. Frostbite and starvation caused his hair, nails, skin, and the entire soles of his feet to fall off during a grueling two-month trek back to camp. At one-point Mawson fell down a crevasse and was left dangling in the abyss from a rope. He dragged his crippled body up and continued on the trek. Mawson's journey has gone down in the annals of polar exploration as probably the most terrible ever undertaken in Antarctica. Yet, when he returned to camp, he sent a message back to his fiancée in Australia. A short message, but one so understated it could only have been written by one of those epic heroes of the age of Antarctic exploration.[1] There was no complaint or self-pity. No mention of the horrors he had just endured. It read, *'Deeply regret delay,' 'Only just managed to reach hut.'* Not only is endurance tribal, the way it is handled in terms of fortitude, grace, and control are important in achieving elusive outcomes.

Patience is perhaps the most understated yet important characteristic of any innovative effort. Great victories take time and that requires patience. Yet, we live in a world of fast results, express shipping, and video on demand. There is nothing wrong with any of those things, in moderation. However, because of those things, we may all be losing the ability to practice patience and the situation may only get worse. We do not like to wait. In fact, patience is often viewed as a sign of weakness. Yet, patience is a hallmark of leading change.[2] Like endurance, patience speaks to how we respond to delay or an undesired consequence. However, with patience it is the emotional response that is in focus. An individual or organization demonstrates patience when it responds to delay or adversity without getting angry or engaging other negative emotional consequences. In an episode of Mr. Rogers Neighborhood, Fred Rogers wanted viewers to hear what it sounded like when the fish in his on-set aquarium ate their food. He called in a marine biologist to install a microphone in the tank, but the biologist grew impatient when the fish were not eating. They could have re-recorded the scene, but Rogers kept it in as a lesson in patience and the appreciation of silence. Patience requires an ability to see things from several perspectives, to remain calm in the face of calamity, and to quickly adjust expectations. Experimentation, scientific problem-solving approaches, and great knowledge flow can assist in developing organizational patience. Also, it is important not to mistake patience for lack of speed. Patience improves speed. Rather than redoing reckless decisions, the organization gets it right the first time.

So, if obstacles are going to appear, is walking through them the only remedy available? Actually, the answer is "no". There is a reactive part of persevering that deals with enduing an obstacle and there is a proactive part that identifies potential obstacles and develops coping strategies. The proactive part is risk management. It is possible to foresee challenges ahead, real and imagined. There can be very obvious gaps in the requirements of an endeavor and an organization's capabilities. It is also possible to see dragons and fire ahead when such things are not a threat. The goal of risk management is to objectively reconcile the requirements with the capabilities and develop a way to cope. This is not easy. There is a tendency to overestimate the capabilities of an organization and underestimate the difficult of an endeavor. There are countless stories of failed software implementations to back up this claim.[3] To persevere, an honest evaluation of an endeavor's riskiness must be made. This serves three purposes. First, the organization can prepare for the challenges ahead. Second, through this process we can understand more about the organization's propensity for taking on risky endeavors. If the endeavors that are attempted are low risk, then there is a strong likelihood of low innovative outcomes. Finally, developing risk profiles of projects allows the organization to track them over time. This gives insight into the organization's capacity to mitigate risk. In the following section, I present a framework for developing and tracking the risk profile of projects.

Risk Management

Risk is an unfortunate but likely consequence of any ambitious endeavor. While there are many stories and articles that tout "fast innovation" and "failing fast", the experiences observed in this research were tedious and cumbersome. They also encountered many setbacks. Importantly, in keeping with the instinct of ambition and success, setbacks are not cast as "failure" and there is no discussion of accepting failure as part of the journey. Rather, it is known by the tribe that there will be tough patches in the road and that patience and perseverance will be required to maintain the journey. As mentioned earlier, new ideas and new frontiers rarely appear as beautiful swans; instead, they are ugly ducklings. It is the goal of the tribe to turn the ugly ducklings into swans. To help in this process, it is useful to categorize an endeavor or project in terms of its predisposition for setbacks. Three broad dimensions of riskiness are:

1. *Structure:* How well understood is the problem? Are there paths of prior success? Has this been done before?
2. *Technological Experience:* Do we have skills, resources, and "know-how" to address the problem?
3. *Scope:* How big is the project? How encompassing is it to the organization? How much resource will be required?

Structure

Structure is a very tricky aspect of riskiness. In many endeavors, the bulk of time and effort is spent solving the problem and a minuscule amount of time is spent in defining the problem. It is also possible to believe that the problem is understood and a recipe is obvious when it is not.[4] In fact, some organizations may define the problem based solely on the recipes that it knows. Further, there is also a mistaken belief that the sooner the project is started, the sooner it will be finished.[5] Speeding toward a solution or defining a problem based on an inventory of known solutions can actually waste time and resources. The magic in structuring the problem is knowing that you need to collect data to define the problem, not define the problem then collect data. It is a small but important nuance. There are a number of tools and techniques that help in this process. I will describe the approach commonly taken in the super projects and innovative organizations I researched. It is illustrated in Figure 7.2. It has a number of similar features as other frameworks, but it is also different in that it simultaneously combines proof of concept with design.

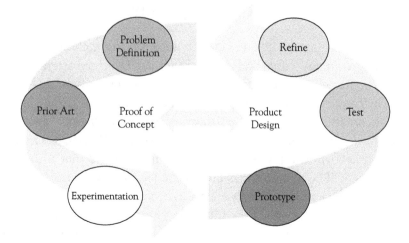

Figure 7.2: Problem Structure: Proof of Concept and Design

The process begins with building a "strawman" or first iteration of the problem definition. Quite likely, this will be stated in terms that are wordy or, too complex. I see this all the time in my consulting endeavors. When I ask an organization what they are trying to achieve the answer is usually a long narrative built on the words "change", "transformation", "velocity", "emerging technology", and "process". There is nothing wrong with any of these terms, but it becomes pretty obvious that there is no definitive problem definition, just buzz words and a lot of PowerPoint slides. A good problem definition is stated in simper terms. For example, Apple's rally cry for iPod and iTunes was to "revolutionize the experience of listening to music". The device and download platform were avenues to achieve the objective, but they were not part of the problem statement. Next, the organization should search for prior art. *Who has done this before? Are there examples we can follow?* Too often the organization assumes that it is the only one to attempt the feat. Also, there is a strong tendency to localize the search for prior art. The search should include other contexts, other organizations, and similar situations that are far afield from the home base. There is a lot of knowledge and a lot of experience that are lost when the search from prior art is localized. Experimentation is the next phase. Here, cause and effect relationships are tested. Various versions of prior art are assessed. Myth is separated from fact. Together, problem definition, prior art, and experimentation provide a proof of concept. Questions such as "*is this the right problem?"*, *"is this important?"*, and *is this achievable?* are addressed and come into focus.

In the design part of the process, the problem definition is operationalized as a project. Tasks, deadlines, sequences of events, all the essential pieces of the puzzle are developed. Prototyping is a critical aspect of this activity. A trial project may be launched, a test product built, or a collaborative arrangement tested. This not only brings an aspect of visualization to the project, it formally tests assumptions and assists in sharpening or redefining the problem statement. Testing extends prototyping by combining and subtracting attributes of various prototypes. The porotypes are also tested against a variety of conditions and constraints. Refinement is the process of improving and clarifying based on the results of testing and prototyping. Existing and new knowledge are then combined to sharpen or reshape the problem definition. Importantly, this should not be a long or laborious process. However, it should be rigorous and should constitute a significant amount of the innovation effort. The interplay of "proof of concept" and "design" provide a useful context for conceptualizing, visualizing, and testing the structure and organizational understanding of the problem.

Technological Experience

Similar to structure, it is very easy to overestimate the organization's experience and capability to meet an innovation challenge. This is particularly true if the challenge lies outside organizational expertise, but the organization does not recognize it as such. Likewise, it is easy to underestimate capability if the challenge is within the organization's expertise but is not recognized as such. Boundaries of expertise change over time, and it is possible for an organization to lose and/or gain expertise unwittingly. If the organization has accurately developed proof of concept and design, then some idea of the skills, technologies, and resources needed should come into focus. Of course, the most readily available source of technological experience is within the organization. *Internal* capabilities can exist or they can be developed or acquired. Some of the world's most incredible inventions were the result of evolved internal capabilities. Flight, electricity, telecommunications, and automobiles were born from the efforts of self-trained inventors and invented organizations. Therefore, it is important to assess what current capabilities are and what they might become. *External* capabilities are those that exist beyond the organization's boundary. It is collaboration or joint venture with organizations that might have the knowledge or capability to push a project forward. In its best form, collaboration can speed up project progress and reduce risk. However, it can also be an impediment if the external organization is not cooperative (read, not tribal) or the project is so specialized that creating shared understanding is difficult. A third source of technological expertise is *combinatorial*. This can be internal or external. It is the resulting expertise or capability that results from combining capabilities. This may be difficult to define but powerful if it is identified. In super projects, where the goal is to deconstruct the human genome, explore Pluto, or photograph a black hole, combinations of expertise are critical. Astronomers, combined with astrophysicists, which are then combined with experts in artificial intelligence, create knowledge and expertise that is beyond any individual person or tribe. Without it, the technical expertise needed for the Event Horizon Telescope cannot be realized. The same is true in projects that develop advanced robotics, genomics, or new treatments for the worst diseases. The right portfolio of internal external, and combinatorial experience is a critical avenue for reducing the riskiness of the most innovative endeavors.

Scope

Another factor of risk is scope. This is the magnitude of the project in terms of budget, time, people, and impact. A great way to think about scope is in terms of *reach* and *range*.[6] If a project encompasses multiple organizations, multiple boundaries, and multiple lines of authority, then reach is high and so is the level of risk. It becomes more difficult to coordinate and build needed systems of technology and process to successfully manage the project. Again, it is easier than one would think to mistake a project that has high reach for one that has low reach. Sometimes, coordinating two autonomous organization is difficult. In addition, it is easy to underestimate where boundaries of autonomy exist within a large organization. Many software implementations have failed miserably because this aspect of scope was not understood. That said, it is also a mistake to scale back a much-needed project because of obstacles in reconciling reach.

Range can be thought of as the magnitude of change or adjustment in methods, work, or process needed to meet the challenge. If existing ways of work will not be unsettled, then the dimension of range is low and so is potential risk. However, if methods, processes, and ways of work will be significantly changed to accommodate the endeavor, then range is high and so is

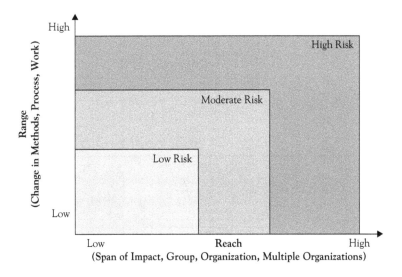

Figure 7.3: Scope as Reach and Range

risk. When reach and range are combined, then a portfolio of possible scope possibilities is revealed. This is illustrated in Figure 7.3. Of course, when reach and range are high, then scope is high and so is potential risk. Conversely, when reach and range are low, then scope is low and so is potential risk. In between is a cautionary frontier where scope is typically moderate. However, it can also drift low or high depending on the organization and the other factors of structure and technological experience.

Once an assessment of scope, structure, and technological experience is complete, then it is possible to frame the overall riskiness of the project. Not only is it a good idea to determine where an individual project falls in terms of risk, it is also useful to plot the project within the portfolio of other organizational projects so that the amount of total risk becomes known. Sometimes, the addition of a risky project will carry the organization to a level of unbearable overall risk. Conversely, the organization might determine that an anticipated project carries little risk and does not add to the total amount of organizational risk. Most importantly, plotting the riskiness of a project can sound the alarm for interventions needed to build a predisposition for eventual success. Using the three dimensions, I have created a project risk portfolio as a tool for planning and managing risk. It is presented in Figure 7.4.

As illustrated, a project will take on a certain "Type" 1–7 based on its position with respect to technological knowledge, problem structure, and

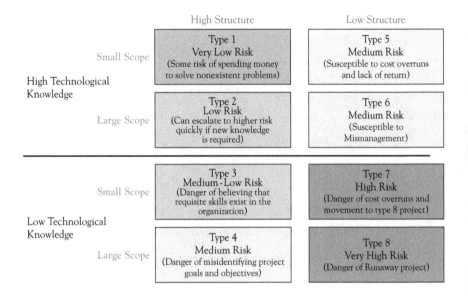

Figure 7.4: Project Risk Portfolio

scope. An interesting characteristic of the super projects I researched was their attention to this aspect of their work. There was a consistent monitoring of a project's status and its progress through the matrix. Also, all projects and even pieces of projects were known in terms of their riskiness. The innovative touch consisted of these seven important rules:

1. Too many Type 7 or 8 projects are trouble.
2. Too many Type 1 or 2 projects are trouble.
3. Type 7 and 8 projects need to be managed toward Type 1 or Type 2.
4. Type 1 and Type 2 projects should not become Type 7 or Type 8.
5. Type 5 and 6 projects are potential opportunities to leverage know-how.
6. Type 3 and Type 4 projects require a "helping hand".
7. Numerous projects clustered northwest, northeast, southeast or southwest may indicate a project management problem.

Keeping the rules in mind, let's take a tour of the project risk portfolio. If a project measures low on problem structure, high on scope, and low on technological skill, then it is the riskiest. We call these Type 8 projects. The organization does not have requisite skills, the problem is not well understood, and the scope is broad. If we change the dimension of scope from large to small, then it becomes a Type 7 project. Scope is smaller but the organization still lacks technological skill and problem definition. The project is still very risky. Both of these projects live in the southeast part of the portfolio. Too many of these projects may tax an organization's endurance. Also, if a project "spins" in the southeast for too long, then it may drain resources from other endeavors. Runaway projects and tied-up resources are a real threat.

It is quite likely that many organizations will "pass" on such projects. Opting instead for something less risky and more of a sure bet. The assumption is that risk is something to be avoided. Ironically, this reasoning may not always be sound; by passing, the organization may be yielding good ground to a rival. Most innovative endeavors begin as Type 7 or Type 8. Of course, a rival will also see the project as Type 8 but, rather than run, they will actively take it on and then reposition it so that it is less of a threat. For example, the iPhone would have initially appeared as a Type 8 project to Apple. At that time, Apple, was not clear about what the market valued (low structure), Apple had few partners or little know-how in telecommunication (low technological skill), and the scope of the project was large. The device was a sea change for the organization. Yet, the company was extremely efficient in deconstructing each risk factor and eventually moving the project to safer ground (Type 1 or 2). In the case of Apple, the structure of the problem seemed to be addressed first. This involved developing an outcome for the project in terms of how people use information and how technology was converging. They then leaped the technological hurdle by partnering with AT&T. Finally, the projects were divided into logical phases and prioritized to meet the challenges of scope.[7] Importantly, there is not one prescribed path in moving a Type 8 project to a Type 1 or Type 2 project. At least I did not see it in my research. However, there is always a concerted effort to "manage" a risky project to safer ground by directly addressing the three dimensions of risk.

If a project measures low on scope, has high structure, and the organization has high technological knowledge, then it is Type 1. These projects are the least risky. If the scope is changed from small to large, then the project is Type 2. The scope is more encompassing, but the risk is still low. The home of these projects is in the northwest frontier of the portfolio. The northwest is a magnet for any organization. It is known as the "home run ball", "the low hanging fruit", or "the no brainer". The organization is skilled, the problem is known, and the scope is manageable. In many organizations I have consulted with, this part of the portfolio is heavily populated, and the innovative drive is to keep adding more. The obvious problem is that at some point the real innovation lies elsewhere. Too many northwest projects are a manifest sign of complacency and, quite simply, a lack of organizational courage. Interestingly when there is a dramatic shift (new chain of logic), these projects can turn into Type 7 and Type 8. This is a definitive outcome of organizations that find themselves in a "World Turned Upside Down". For example, the projects in retail that were low risk Type 1 and 2 for Sears became riskier when online retailing shifted the marketplace. To be balanced, Type 1 and Type 2 projects can be great endeavors. Sometimes, just a tweak or a minor adjustment is all that is needed for a great strategic endeavor. However, too many Type 1 or Type 2 projects may narrow the vision of the organization and the skill sets needed to take on more difficult endeavors. I think about this every time I visit a United States post office.

A project that measures high in technological knowledge, low in scope, and low in problem structure is Type 5. If the scope turns from small to large, then it is Type 6. These projects occupy the northeast part of the portfolio. This space is a conundrum for organizations. The technological know-how exists but the problem definition is not clear. These projects can be considered moderately risky. However, they can be really important if you are the first organization to shift the project from the northeast to the northwest. I saw a lot of these instances in a research project I conducted on technologies remaking the world.[8] Some firms had extreme know-how but were unable to fully use it because the application cases were unclear. This was particularly true in the area of artificial intelligence and block chain technologies. The dot-com bubble and crash of 2000 were largely a result of technical know-how seeking an unclear problem definition.[9] However, once the problem definition was solved, then the project became a strategic strike. This is commonly found in the field of medicine. Dr. Jonas Salk successfully combined and extended the efforts of other research teams in the search for a vaccine for polio. In the two years before the vaccine was widely available, there were more than 45,000 cases of polio in the United States—this number dropped to 910 in 1962.[10] His main contribution was shaping the problem such that know-how could be applied. And, that is the key, problem definition; if it is wrong or remains undermined for too long, then mismanagement and excessive costs can occur. However, if the problem definition is shaped correctly, then the organization finds new avenues to transfer and further wield its technological know-how.

If technological knowledge is low, problem structure is high, and scope is high, then the project is Type 4. Again, this has moderate risk. The project is not something consistent with organizational skills and the larger scope adds to the complexity. If we shift the scope from large to small, the risk is reduced, and the project becomes Type 3. As implied, when working in the lower end of the technological skill frontier, a great avenue in reducing risk is to scope the project smaller. However, repeatedly applying this strategy may result in projects with limited impact. A better approach is to reduce scope with an eye toward gaining requisite skills and then moving the project to Type 2. Together, Type 3 and Type 4 projects occupy the southwest frontier of the portfolio. Again, this is a paradoxical and sometimes frustrating area because the organization understands the problem definition but does not have the know-how to proceed without risk. The organization also faces a temptation to believe they have the skills just because they understand the domain of the problem. Perhaps the best way forward is to recognize these projects as needing a "helping hand". Collaboration with other organizations can quickly move the project to the safer ground of the northwest. However, if the partnering organization adds complexity and does not share the same understanding of the problem, then the project can quickly shift to the risky frontier of south-east or the northeast. Skills can also be developed within the organization to move a project to safer ground. If this can be done quickly and effectively, then the technological know-how line can shift down trading risky frontier of the south for safer frontier in the north. The Wright Brothers followed this approach. They were self-educated and methodical and moved the technological experience line downward. Samuel Langley, the Wright Brothers rival, moved the technological know-how line upward with his efforts and approach. The more Langley experimented, the less he knew! This was ironic, given that Langley had the resources of the Smithsonian Institution and well-trained scientists at his behest. Through what they learned, the Wright Brothers were able to bring definition to the problem, deconstruct the project, and realize success.

Patience, persistence, and endurance are the tougher side of the innovation conversation. Yet, psychologists tell us that during those trying times, we are experiencing the times of our lives. Somehow, we persevere. Organizations may also experience key inflection points in their progressions. In such times, it is tempting to run or ignore the challenge. A Tribal approach not only faces adversity, it expects it, and welcomes it. That is certainly different from a perspective that cultivates a subtle fear of environmental uncertainty, high-velocity environments, and the unexpected. There is an unmistakable aggressiveness in tackling challenges and an unmistakable sense of honor in meeting the challenges within a tribe. Knowing that innovation is risky is the first step in building organizational courage. This can be done very methodically by examining scope, problem structure, and technical knowledge. Then, coping strategies and interventions can be developed to move a risky endeavor to a less risky frontier. This greatly enhances the predisposition for a successful outcome. Sometimes change requires more than authority, a vision statement, or PowerPoint slides. It requires a "gut check" of an organization's perseverance and a strategy for moving projects through the project risk portfolio.

Notes

1. Bear Grylls, *True Grit*. Bantam Press, 2013.
2. Christina Bielaszka-DuVernay, "The Balance Needed to Lead Change," *Harvard Business Review*, September 16, 2008.
3. A. H. Segars and D. Chaterjee, "Diets that Don't Work: Where Enterprise Planning Goes Wrong," *Wall Street Journal*, August 23, 2010.
4. Dwayne Spradlin, "Are You Solving the Right Problem?" *Harvard Business Review*, September 2012.
5. Strefan Thomke and Donald Reinerstsen, "Six Myths of Product Development," *Harvard Business Review*, May 2012.
6. Peter Keen, *Shaping the Future: Business Design Through Information Technology*. Boston, MA: Harvard Business School Press, 1991.
7. Brian Merchant, *The One Device: The Secret history of the iPhone*. Little, Brown and Company, 2017.
8. Albert H. Segars, "Seven Technologies Remaking the World," *Sloan Management Review*, March 2019.
9. Ben Geier, "What did we Learn From the Dot Com Bubble of 2000?" *Time*, March 12, 2015.
10. Salk Institute for Biological Sciences. History of Salk: About Jonas Salk. Salk Institute website. https://www.salk.edu/about/history-of-salk/jonas-salk/. Accessed June 27, 2019.

· 8 ·

SACRIFICE

Human progress is neither automatic nor inevitable … Every step toward the goal of justice requires sacrifice, suffering, and struggle; the tireless exertions and passionate concern of dedicated individuals.

— Dr. Martin Luther King, Jr.

Sacrifice is likely the most personal and deeply emotional of the instincts. Almost everyone has a story of sacrifice. A loved one that lost their life in war, a parent that worked two or three jobs to provide, and the time we gave up our place in line for someone who needed it more. In my opinion, these selfless acts may be the most beautiful part of life and living. They are also extremely tribal. I remember walking to my office at UNC one beautiful fall morning. Ahead of me were two of our graduate students. The night before had been blustery and stormy. As they walked, the students passed several pieces of trash scattered along the ground. This was the harmless kind of trash: paper, cups, plastic bottles, and cans. Nothing gooey or repulsive. Now, I am far from perfect, but I was one of many in the post-boomer generation that were heavily influenced by the "Keep America Beautiful" public service announcement that was launched in 1971.[1] In the commercial, Iron Eyes Cody, an American Indian, cries at the sight of trash in the rivers and landscape of America. Since seeing that commercial as a child, I pick up trash. I drove my friends and parents crazy, but I am proud to say they eventually got the spirit. So, on that fall day, I stopped and began picking up the trash in the walkway. I was quickly assisted by a few undergraduate students as the graduate students walked on. An hour later, those same two graduate students appeared in my office. At the time, I was the lead faculty member of the sustainability program at the Kenan-Flagler Business School. The students were there to complain about our program. They wanted to "change the world" and they thought the school was not thinking big enough about the topic. No one seemed to care about sustainability, except them. This was quite stunning, given that our program was top ranked, and our students were well known for their community service. I could not help thinking about what I observed earlier in the day. Maybe picking up some trash wasn't big enough for them, but it was something they "passed" on. Something some good-natured undergraduate students and I did not "pass" on. Now, these two graduate students were smart and dutiful, maybe just a bit self-absorbed. I listened, helped them, and promised we would do better. I did not mention what I witnessed earlier in the day. However, it did occur to me that, while good intentioned and ambitious, they lacked tribal spirit. It is a small sacrifice to stop and pick up some wayward debris, but it demonstrates a concern for the tribe and the greater good above the concern for one's self. Maybe you can change the world with small kindnesses. This is the heart and soul of this important instinct. Let's look at it from an individual perspective and an organizational perspective.

Personal Sacrifice

From an individual perspective, there is a duty and an expectation to sacrifice for the tribe. This is important, sacrifice is reciprocal, one lays aside their interests for the greater good, and it is also expected that others in the tribe will do the same. As part of the research for this book, interviews and surveys were used to identify these sacrifices. In some sense, you can think of these as the "cost" of being part of a tribe. They are:

1. **Time**—Spending time to complete tasks, help others, help yourself.
2. **Wealth**—Sharing rewards, working for purpose, alternative rewards.
3. **Plans**—Working on the tribe's schedule and not your own.
4. **Talents**—Giving your talents to enrich others, bending your talents.
5. **Energy**—Giving the most physical and mental effort to the task.
6. **Pride**—Letting go of opinions, humbleness, earning the conversation.
7. **Fame**—Sharing credit, spotlight accomplishments before people.

Let's discuss these attributes within the context of some extraordinary examples of personal sacrifice. Dashrath Manjhi is known as the "Mountain Man".
He was born in a Musahar family, at the lowest rung of India's caste system.
He ran away from his home at a young age and worked at Dhanbad's coal
mines. After many years, he returned to his village and married Falguni Devi.
Tragically, she died while trying to cross a rocky mountain that separated her
village from the village that had medical facilities. Because he did not want
anyone else to experience such a fate, Manjhi decided to carve a path through
the Gehlour hills so that his village would have easier access to medical care.
Using a hammer and chisel, He carved a path 360 ft. long, 25 ft. deep, and 30
ft. wide to form a road through the rocks in Gehlour hill. He completed the
work in 22 years (1960–1982). Though mocked for his efforts, Manjhi's work
has made life easier for the people of his village. The sacrifices of time, wealth,
and energy are paramount in this example. A 22-year endeavor is an amazing
amount of personal sacrifice just to ensure that fellow villagers have a path to
the nearest hospital. There is also a sacrifice of personal gain because the time
pursing other enriching endeavors are eclipsed by the time needed for the
task. Of course, it takes an amazing amount of physical energy to chisel away
at the rock but it also takes an enormous amount of psychological energy to
keep going. Granted, this is an extreme case but it illustrates the depth and
types of sacrifice that some make for a task they truly see as important. Of
particular note is the amount of time and psychological and physical energy
needed for things beyond the ordinary. Sometimes, these unglamorous aspects
of innovative efforts are often not highlighted in books or in motivational
speeches. Yet, for those that do sacrifice, it is often done without fanfare; and,
if it is recalled, it is said to have been well worth it.

Often noted in interviews and very prominent in the surveys is the notion
of humbleness and sharing the spotlight. In a sense, the pursuit of individual
fame or of recognition is seen as harmful to a tribal effort. Again, an example
highlights this important point. Although he eventually achieved a well-de-
served place in history, Martin Luther King Jr. was not on a quest for fame
or fortune. From the earliest weeks of the Montgomery bus boycott (1955–
1956), he saw his role as one of personal sacrifice. He was drafted by the other
African-American civic activists in Montgomery to be the spokesperson for
the bus boycott, primarily because he was brand-new in town and was not
aligned with any of the existing civic factions in the city. Throughout his
time as leader, Dr. King frames his life and his role in a self-sacrificial way.
"Bearing the cross" is the phrase that he uses on at least four or five occasions

that are recorded on audiotape—where he is explicitly or implicitly talking about how he copes with the role he was given but did not seek.[2] Dr. King gave his talents, time, and energy fully and willingly and endured the ultimate personal sacrifice for an extraordinary cause in a very difficult time. One of his underlying themes was that of humility. He knew that a humble person does not compare themselves with others. It is the expectations of one's self and self-improvement that are the most important gauges. Having a realistic sense of one's position relative to other people is important. As practiced by King, humility devoid of any arrogance is liberating and powerful. As noted by the gestalt therapist Fritz Perls,[3] "*I am I and you are you; I am not in this world to live up to your expectations, and you are not in this world to live up to mine*". This perspective is a critical part of sacrifice and essential for climbing emotional, political, and organizational mountains.

As both of these examples illustrate, sacrifice begins with a commitment of time. Accomplishing worthwhile goals will likely take more time than one would like to give. It takes time to accomplish your goals, and there is also the time that you spend helping others and the time you spend improving your own skills. This certainly does not imply that time as a quantity is the answer. It is the amount of "quality" time that is important. So, while there is an expectation of a time commitment, tribes understand that the time must be used efficiently and effectively. As Dr. King knew, spending energy in a way that promoted humility and reconciliation was more effective than open warfare. It was a quicker means to the mark. Wealth is also something that is sacrificed for bigger ideas. Now, I am not talking about socialism or a complete lack of concern for wealth and well-being. I am talking about the recognition of limited resources and the benefits of being rewarded fairly and having those who play critical roles being rewarded fairly. An example helps clarify this point. As quarterback for the Baltimore Ravens, Joe Flacco was part of a Super Bowl winning football team and the most valuable player of the Super Bowl. He was rewarded with one of the most lucrative contracts in professional sports. Unfortunately, the aftermath was not so glamorous. Flacco and the team began a free-fall after the Super Bowl win. The high price paid to Flacco left limited room for the acquisition and development of key players. Mainly, an offensive line to protect the quarterback and a defense to prevent the other team from scoring.[4] Yes, there are stars in super projects and in innovative organizations but they recognize the key contributions of other tribal members and the benefits of sacrificing some short-term wealth for the long-term benefits of greater accomplishment. Back to the football example, this is one of the greatest lessons learned from Tom Brady of the New England Patriots. One of the most celebrated and accomplished quarterbacks in NFL history (three league MVPs, winner of six Super Bowls, and winner of four Super Bowl MVPs); he is willing to sign contracts with the Patriots for less money than he can receive on the open market. This leaves resources to develop a team that wins and wins for a long time.[5] Love them or hate them, the Patriots have been very tribal during their incredible run.[6]

Willingness to change or completely eliminate one's plans is a subtle but important part of sacrifice. As noted earlier, Martin Luther King had no aspiration for leading an effort such as the Civil Rights Movement. Dashrath Manjhi had no original aspiration to build a road. The willingness to be adaptable and flexible with your own sequence of timelines and desired destinations is very tribal. It is not easy to accomplish, and it may run counter to our own "being" but it is necessary. Innovation rarely adjusts to your schedule. In one of the projects researched for this book, there is a wall mural of the expected path. The depiction is neat, logical, and very organized. On the next wall is a mural of the path as it has unfolded. This depiction looks more like a spider web or a tangled fishing line. It is a point of humor and a clever reminder of how plans are sometimes sacrificed.

Talents and energy are also personal sacrifices that build the overall capability of the tribe. Sacrificing talent is taking the things in which we excel and using them to help build the talents of others. Mentoring is the activity associated with this sacrifice. Conveying wisdom, know-how, and experiences face-to-face in field conditions is perhaps the best transfer of knowledge and talent between two individuals. If we elevate this activity to interchange between groups of individuals or tribes, then the benefit is multiplied. It takes time and willingness to share one's talents for this to happen, but it is something very tribal. I certainly benefitted from mentors who were willing to share their skill and insights with me. I never thought about that as a sacrifice until I began doing the same for my students. Yet, I never regret the time I spent; and, hopefully, those experiences were beneficial. I know they were to me.

Along with talents, energy is a needed sacrifice. Great feats are tiring no matter who you are and what your age is. It is important to be "present" with mental energy and active in terms of physical energy. There is the heavy lifting in the accomplishment of one's own task, and there is the heavy lifting in helping others accomplish their tasks when needed. William Harvey Carney was the first African-American awarded the United States Congressional Medal of Honor. He was born a slave in Virginia, but eventually made his way to freedom in Massachusetts. When the Union Army began accepting volunteers, he joined the 54th Massachusetts Infantry Regiment, the first African-American unit organized by the northern states. The 54th Massachusetts Infantry Regiment, led by Robert Gould Shaw, was tasked with taking Fort Wagner, a beachhead fortification that guarded the southern approach to Charleston Harbor. A previous attack on the fort failed, and the 54th was chosen for the next attempt. As the soldiers stormed the fort's walls, the Union flag bearer was killed. Carney grabbed the flag and held it for the duration of the battle. Carney, along with the rest of the 54th, was forced to retreat. Throughout the battle Carney never lost possession of the flag, despite suffering multiple injuries. *"Boys, I only did my duty; the old flag never touched the ground!"* he said after the battle. Carney was awarded the Medal of Honor in 1900.

Pride is a difficult sacrifice. Yet, Dr. King rallied people in the streets, suffered indignation, and encountered ridicule. Fellow villagers mocked and ridiculed Dashrath Manjhi as he built a road for their benefit. Innovative organizations are filled with incredibly talented people. They are also people that gladly sacrifice pride for the benefit of the tribe. This means supporting the idea that is not your own, looking past the mistakes of others, knowing there is always more to learn and earning the conversation. It is tempting for all of us to believe we are worthy of more than we receive. As educators and researchers, we see this from time to time. Newly graduated students who feel that their degree and their insights make them immediately ready to be the chief executive officer. Academics who believe their research unlocks the key that is unseen by even the wisest politicians or judges. In the broader context of media and news reporting, the panel of talking heads searching for the catch phrase that launches their own show. It is life. However, in a tribal organization there is a strong theme of "earning the conversation". This means having accomplishments, experiences, and trials that qualify a person to be a part of the "conversation". Your works give your words "iron". It has nothing to do with age, rank, or years of employment. It is based on the record of accomplishment. Tribal councils were populated by elders and young warriors who had "earned the conversation". This along with tolerance and a strong sense of advocacy for the best ideas, wherever they come from, are the bedrock of sacrificing pride.

Fame is the final of the individual sacrifices. Importantly, this is not to say that people in innovative organizations do not want fame; they do. However, the fame they seek is for the project, the project's goal, and for the team, not for themselves. This can be difficult to accomplish because the great inno-vation narrative is that "someone" came up the great idea, created the inno-vation, and will likely, once again, "walk on water" in the near future. We love our heroes and we love the myth of the lone genius. Even in one of the projects researched for this book, a young scientist, Katie Baumon, became the unwitting face of the Event Horizon Telescope. Social media posts by uninformed politicians, media jocks, internet influencers, as well as dramatic and exaggerated news stories went "viral" amplifying her role and de-amplify-ing the role of other project members.[7] Importantly, Dr. Baumon did not ask for any of it; in fact, she has always been steadfast in her claim that the effort was collective. Most importantly, in the best example of a tribal mindset, her colleagues at MIT quickly came to her defense, acknowledging her import-ant contributions and also echoing the sentiment that the feat could only be accomplished with a collective effort. Therein lies some of the elusive story behind innovation. It is a typically a collective effort of very intelligent, inno-vative, and humble minds that are bound by the drive and thrill of chasing the impossible.

Organizational Sacrifice

Now, let's raise the level of analysis just a bit. How do organizations embody the instinct of sacrifice? While we all have experienced or witnessed some form of individual sacrifice, organizational sacrifices are not as well docu-mented or as well understood. Yet, they do occur. Plus, they occur much more naturally and much less painfully in innovative organizations. To them, orga-nizational sacrifice is part of the hunt. The instinct can be found in a phone conversation between Steve Jobs of Apple and Nike CEO, Mark Parker. After assuming leadership of Nike, Parker asked Jobs if he had any advice. *"Well, just one thing,"* said Jobs. *"Nike makes some of the best products in the world. Products that you lust after. But you also make a lot of crap. Just get rid of the crappy stuff and focus on the good stuff."* Jobs paused, and Parker filled the quiet with a chuckle; however, Jobs didn't laugh. He was serious. *"He was absolutely right,"* said Parker. *"We had to edit."*[8] Napoleon practiced this same mode of organiza-tional efficiency in his Grand Arme'e. Napoleon's forces traveled with small logistical trains to improve mobility. His soldiers learned that marauding was a more reliable source of food, horses, and provisions than the traditional sup-ply system. They endured the hardships of traveling light for the advantage of mobility and adaptability. Often hungry, they were eager to fight for the glory of France and were the most feared force in Europe.[9]

Sacrifice is not a term that is typically associated with exploring new frontiers or generating fantastic ideas. However, it is a strong tribal instinct and it is also a critical component of successful innovation. Sacrifice is the ultimate act of organizational selflessness; rather than do what is best for a powerful member or an influential sub-group, decisions are based on benefitting the entire tribe. Beyond this, decisions are based on what will make the tribe viable in the future rather than what has made the tribe viable in the past. Therefore, it is this act of sacrifice that sheds or deescalates non-performing initiatives and replaces them with new, more promising, initiatives. Organizations without this instinct may add new initiatives or programs of change but they never sacrifice the original initiatives that these new projects are designed to replace. This results in a "crowded house" of failed or underperforming initiatives as well as the new initiatives that were launched to replace them. Such crowding can create the dangerous paradox of "*Everything is Important, and Nothing is Important*". In this context, crowding may starve off resources needed for the successful launch of new initiatives or the required upkeep of performing initiatives. In turn, non-performing initiatives may receive too much resource. When this occurs, the organization may lose its focus and sense of direction as it plants one foot firmly in the past while the other foot timidly steps toward the future. Organizations with a tribal instinct of sacrifice think of innovation not only as the launch of new initiatives but also as the "letting go" of some "non-performing" initiatives.

Organizations in Context

So, now that we have established a definition of organizational sacrifice, the question becomes, "*How do we accomplish it?*" Glad you asked. This is something that I have spent over twenty years helping organizations accomplish. From the Department of Defense, to media concerns, to cutting-edge technology companies, it is a difficult task. Not because it is difficult to know what is "crappy", to use the terminology of the late Steve Jobs, but because it is difficult to say "goodbye". It is never easy to "vote" something off the island, even if it is to make room for something everyone knows is needed. What is needed is a tool and technique to frame the difficult conversation. A way to examine the working parts of the organization in context and then assess if

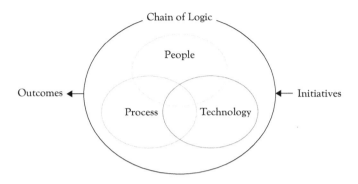

Figure 8.1: An Organization in Context

those parts are "crappy" or "repairable", or "strategic". First, let's build a view of an organization in context.

As illustrated in Figure 8.1, an organization in context consists of two main parts. One of those parts is tangible and observable. It can be thought of as the "engine" of the organization. Organizational theorists call it structure.[10] In the illustration below, it is depicted by the three interlocking rings of *process*, *people*, and *technology*. The second part of an organization is more cerebral, the chain of logic. As developed earlier, this is the initiatives, outcomes, and system of analytical coordination of the organization. It can be thought of as the "compass". Together these parts drive the organization and navigate its path. Ideally, there should be complete consistency between the two parts. However, conditions can change these relationships and many times those shifts require sacrifice. First, let's take a look at the engine.

Process

A process is the sequence of actions or required steps to achieve a particular end. Of course, it is something we are familiar with, but in this context, it takes on a slightly different interpretation. In an organizational context it is the collection of practices, policies, and structures that coordinate activity. In some sense, it is how we are organized for competition. How decisions are made, how functions are organized, reward systems, hiring, procurement, payments, rules, policies, procedures and anything that coordinates the work and activities of the organization are part of "process". To simplify the depiction of process, it is sometimes useful to classify them in broader terms. For example, a manufacturing organization might have broad classes of procurement, logistics, inventory, and manufacturing processes.[11] In addition, they might have back office processes of accounting, human resources, and payroll as well as front office processes of selling and administration. There are many ways to identify and classify processes; the main point is to build some framework for understanding this important part of the engine. As we will see in the next section, doing so helps in determining their usefulness and current contribution.

People

People are an important part of the engine. Of course, we can organize people by their specialty. This is the traditional way of coordinating in many organizations including academia. Each member has a "department" that "fits" their background and specialty. In a business school, these departments are typically marketing, finance, accounting, operations, and, a catch all, management. To keep family peace, every department should have the equal number of people and the same budget. Over the years, I have noticed that this mode of organizing is very beneficial to academics but a little non-beneficial to students. Topics such as international business, entrepreneurship, healthcare, technology management, and innovation have no natural home in the structure. In those instances, there may be stress between the organization of people and needed outcomes. In universities, this usually results in a committee which is a surefire way to kill any innovation. In my consulting and life outside of academia, I have seen the same fate befall many organizations. Perhaps the better way to think about people is in terms of their capabilities. What talents, background, experiences and potential contributions does this person possess? Not, does this person fit neatly in a particular playground? More and more, individuals create identities for themselves beyond degrees and classrooms. This was something very noticeable in super projects and very innovative organizations. Compartmentalization of talent is something that is avoided. It harkens back to the instinct of roles and responsibilities. Therefore, how we view and organize the "people" part of the engine is critically important in assessing its present state.

Technology

Technology represents the tools used to create "leverage" in the engine. In other words, it is those things we use to extend the capabilities of the people and the process. Digital technology, buildings, infrastructure, ground/air transportation as well as how they are used are part of this domain. Technology is tricky because it changes faster than the other parts of the engine. Plus, as illustrated, the three parts of the engine are interlinked. Therefore, as technology changes, then people and process must adapt, and vice versa. Therein lies one major problem within an organizational engine. The adoption of new technology may not guarantee realization of its fullest use. Processes tend to benefit some organizational members and sacrificing those when new technologies dictate such a change might be resisted. As I learned in years of consulting, bad processes benefit somebody; nothing is designed by happenstance. This is the reason the instinct of sacrifice is so very important. The engine of an organization cannot become so sacred that adaptation becomes problematic when new technologies appear on the horizon. The technological leverage of the engine is powerful. Yet, achieving that leverage means shedding old technologies and old process seamlessly and with enthusiasm. To sabotage or obstruct is to become an organizational mob or a collection of rogue actors. To face this fearlessly is to be tribal. The first step in achieving the feat is to create a frame for identifying technology and how it is used within the organization. Classes of systems, classes of technologies, the primary purpose of the technology and/or the organizational placement of the technology are useful means of building this perspective.

Chain of Logic

The second part of an organization in context is the compass or the chain of logic. This concept was discussed in Chapter 6. Now, we can combine the ideas of shifting outcomes and adapting chains of logic to the underlying engine of the organization. In some instances, a shift in outcome not only requires a new chain of logic, it might also require a new configuration of process, technology, and people. However, it might also require that some processes, technologies, and people be completely sacrificed or refitted. It is a burden to carry failing chains of logic and organizational engines as a "safety". Doing so taxes the resources of the organization and causes confusion. As stated by the Roman philosopher Seneca, "*If a man does not know what port he is steering for, no wind is favorable*". If a new and beneficial chain of logic is discovered and communicated, it is much easier to adjust the engine. In fact, if the organization is adaptable, the engine may begin adjusting itself. However, if conflicting, yet coexisting chains seem prominent in the organization, then the engine has no chance of adjusting. It is analogous to automobile being asked to travel to two opposing destinations at the same time. Therefore, it is important to link the engine with the compass.

Ok, we just spent a few paragraphs identifying the two main pieces of an organization and emphasizing the importance of identifying and categorizing the component parts. There are three reasons for doing so. First, it is important to see the interconnections between the compass and the engine of an organization. My experiences and research lead me to believe that organizational leaders sometimes focus on one or the other rather than the combination. Second, categorizing the parts of the engine helps shape a picture of how the organization has invested its resources. Every part of the engine as well as every chain of logic is an investment. Time, money, and the opportunity cost of other paths are embedded in these components. If we can frame the components, then we can begin to assign costs. Finally, we can build a portfolio that assesses the strategic importance today and in the future of the component parts. Here, we determine what is really important in terms of cost and strategic importance. Once the portfolio is built, then we can start the process of determining where to invest resources and where we take away resources. The hard task of sacrifice begins in earnest; I call it *Investment Triage*.

Investment Triage

A useful way to unlock the *"Everything is Important, and Nothing is Important"* paradox is to think about organizational sacrifice as a form of investment triage. An organization must determine what is most important for competitive survival. The organization must also realistically determine what is less important, what might need a refit, and what may need to be sacrificed completely. The "what" are the parts of the organizational engine. The context for determining importance is the organizational compass. Processes, technologies, and people (capabilities) must be scrutinized for their "strategic importance". Strategic importance speaks to the criticalness of the engine part in achieving significant and important objectives. This assessment is done against the backdrop of emerging and established chains of logic. A process, technology, or capability may measure "low" in strategic importance, meaning that it is not that critical in driving a chain of logic. Alternatively, it may measure "high", meaning that it is extremely critical. Further, this judgment should be made based on today's landscape as well as the landscape of the future.

Depending up on these appraisals, processes, technologies, and capabilities will fall in one of four quadrants:

1. **Legacy:** Low strategic importance now, low in the future.
2. **Falling Star:** High strategic importance now, low in the future.
3. **Rising Star:** Low strategic importance now, high in the future.
4. **Star:** High strategic importance now, high in the future.

Once the matrix is populated, it is then possible to have meaningful conversations about current and future investment. The investment triage matrix is illustrated in Figure 8.2.

Let's walk through the process with a real example from my research and consulting. The United States Navy found itself at a strategic crossroad in the mid- to late 2000s. The assets and technologies of the service were some of the best in the world. However, the engagements these assets were built for were quickly giving way to a very different theater of warfare. The shallow water of the Persian Gulf and the need for mobility and quick strikes were not in the design vision of navy architects. Using investment triage, flag officers categorized ships, submarines, and a host of other technologies as either *Legacy, Falling Star, Rising Star,* or *Star.* I moderated the discussion and occasionally hid behind the podium; it was a very professional but heated discussion. After hours of debate, it was determined that everything the navy

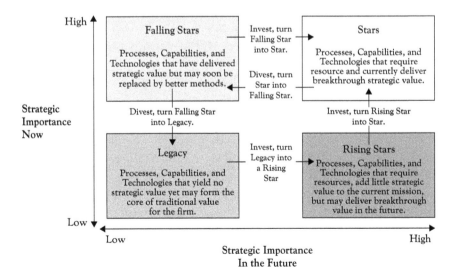

Figure 8.2: Investment Triage Matrix

owned was a *Star* and that it was the army that really needed this exercise. This was not a surprising outcome. It is very tough to acknowledge that the carrier you commanded might be a *Falling Star*. After a week of cooling off and with encouragement from very senior command, the officers returned and did an incredible job of building the portfolio. Not only did they determine that a lot of investment was locked in *Legacy* and *Falling Stars*, they recognized that needed *Rising Star* projects were underfunded. This effort is still underway in the navy.[12]

I tell this story to illustrate three points: First, this aspect of sacrifice may be the hardest part of innovation. These are tough discussions and not something that resolves itself in one meeting. However, with the help of the triage matrix and some general criteria, these discussions can be organized and productive. The common language of *Star*, *Falling Star*, *Legacy*, and *Rising Star* is useful in framing and thinking about organizational assets. Second, the triage matrix links patterns of investment to the compass or chain of logic. Points of consistency and inconsistency are more easily identified. For the navy, a different chain of logic was emerging, something that implied a different pattern of investment. Third, investment priority should shift from Falling Stars and Legacy to Stars and Rising Stars. In addition, some Legacy assets may need to be "voted off the island". This is a very hard discussion. However, the funding needed for emerging *Rising Stars* and *Stars* typically comes from divestment in *Legacy* and *Falling Stars*. This was certainly true for the navy. It was not just a matter of money; the organization needed to focus and gain a shared understanding of priorities. As one admiral noted, "*We can only fit so many cars in the garage*". With that context in mind, let's take a closer look at each of the quadrants.

Legacy

A capability, process, or technology (anything you wish to examine) that is low in strategic importance today and tomorrow is a *Legacy*. This does not necessarily imply that it is something that has been in existence for a long time. Rather, it recognizes that the asset will not yield a clear strategic advantage. Also, it does not mean that the asset is something that is undesirable. Many organizations have legacy products and legacy ways of doing business that are necessary and yield solid flows of cash. Some of these assets may provide a financial and operational foundation for the organization. It does imply that investment in *Legacy* initiatives should be closely monitored and their investment levels should not endanger more important initiatives in the portfolio. In many organizations, *Legacy* initiatives take on mythical status although they have long lost their strategic potential. Therefore, it is easy to mistake *Legacy* assets for *Star* or *Falling Star*. An example that comes to mind is professional athletes, in particular, those in Major League Baseball. Because of past glory and star power, some players may be compensated as a *Star* when their current performance is that of a *Legacy or Falling Star*. This robs the organization of money to find the next Rising Star or keep the current Star.[13] Businesses make the same mistakes with products, political campaigns make the mistake with campaigning, and, as I am reminded by daughter, dads make the same mistake with clothing. Legacy assets can be useful, and in some instances, they can be turned into a Rising Star with some investment. A professor who taught a Legacy course in an academic area under my watch once came to me seeking money to completely modify her course. The course she taught was business law. A useful course but not something that would distinguish our school from any other school. She wanted to build a course on international contracting and negotiation, with an emphasis on Asia Pacific. She had expertise in this area and was looking to do more with her class. I spent the money and her course turned into a Rising Star on the first offering. It eventually became a Star. On the other side of the equation, I was not hesitant to let some legacy faculty "walk" when they demanded an exorbitant "match" from a rival university. I was able to saddle a rival with an overpriced faculty and use the money I saved to chase the next Rising Star.

Falling Stars

A process, technology, or capability that is strategically important today but less strategically important in the future is a *Falling Star*. Because of their importance today, these assets often draw too much investment and a forlorn hope that their fall will be far off into the future. Too often, the fall occurs sooner than expected and investment that should be working toward more promising assets is locked into fading or strategically dead initiatives (the left-hand portion of the matrix). As mentioned earlier, Legacy and Falling Stars are the hardest to recognize because of their history within the organization and their past success. The minivan is a very recent example of a Falling Star product. The minivan's share of the overall U.S. market has steadily decreased within the past decade. SUVs, many of which now offer seating for seven or more people, are attracting many would-be minivan buyers who want a more ruggedly styled vehicle. Something different from the "soccer mom" vehicle they rode in as child.[14] True to form, automobile companies have attempted to make the minivan sleeker and more edgy, to no avail. Rather than pour money into a Falling Star, it may better to divest, let the minivan fall to Legacy, then take the savings and find the next Rising Star. This highlights an important aspect of the matrix. Shifting outcomes cause assets to move. For example, changing tastes and emerging trends have moved the minivan from Star to Falling Star. Investment by the organization can also move assets around in the matrix. Sometimes, it may be possible to invest and move a Falling Star to a Star. Alternatively, the organization can divest of the Falling Star and let the asset fall to Legacy.

Rising Stars

Rising Stars are initiatives that are not strategically important today, but they will become strategically important in the future. In contrast to Falling Stars, organizations will typically underinvest in Rising Stars. This represents short-term thinking and perhaps an unwillingness to take on new initiatives that may seem risky. Instead of moving investment from left to right in the matrix, it may seem practical to "double down" on Legacy and/or Falling Stars in the hope that they find past glory. In doing so, three negative consequences occur: (1) Rising Stars may never receive needed resources, (2) an important inroad of innovation is ignored, and (3) an important strategic inroad is left open to rivals. Rising Stars frequently do not appear as well-formed fantastic new ideas. In contrast, they may seem threatening, ugly, and risky (a Type 8 project). This makes investment extremely difficult; however, success in finding and building a Rising Star reaps many rewards. These are the future stars. A sure sign of a less innovative organization is the absence of Rising Stars. I call the upside-down "L" pattern. There will be some Stars, more Falling Stars, and a lot of Legacy. In these cases, the organization may have a problem identifying important initiatives and needed assets on the horizon. Very innovative organizations will have a balance of assets throughout the matrix. In addition, the trigger for shifts in these assets will be investment and divestment rather than a push from outside environmental or competitive conditions.

Stars

Stars are processes, capabilities, and technologies that are important today and tomorrow. Of course, every organization would like to have as many Stars as possible. However, Stars are hard-won, and when they reach their potential, they require resources to keep their luster. Unfortunately, it is also easy for a Star to drift into the zone of a Falling Star as rivals craft their own solutions to address the prevailing opportunity. Ironically, a Star may fade simply because the organization does not recognize it as a Star. It is not the success the organization wants. Let me give an example. A global textile firm hired me to present the triage matrix to leaders of its multiple business units. After the presentation, the CEO wanted the executives to map the organization's businesses into the matrix. The first presenter was the head of "flags and banners". As he approached the podium to talk about the business and present his financials, a leader of another business unit, "marine and sailcloth", said, "We can skip this presentation. Everyone knows the flags and banner business is legacy." The head of "flags and banners" presented the financials and the future growth in the business. It was definitely a Star. Needless to say, after that presentation, the atmosphere of the room got very serious. The numbers of "marine and sailcloth" were a Falling Star at best. "Technical fabrics" was a runaway Star, yet, the organization was not investing to take advantage of that emerging, and profitable marketplace. The irony is that the less glamorous businesses were the real stars of the organization. The next year, investment was adjusted accordingly, and the firm realized a commanding position in its Star markets. The moral the story is that Stars may not always be "Hollywood" glamorous. Chasing the success where it is rather than where you want it to be can be a significant challenge.

As discussed, the giving and taking away of investment dollars and resources are the key to successful investment triage. Stars and Rising Stars require resource slack. Falling Stars and Legacy initiatives require resource control. There are instances when investment in a Legacy or a Falling Star can result in a new Rising Star or Star; however, it is typically the case that investment flows out of the left side of the matrix and into the right side. While conceptually easy, this is the toughest of the instincts to implement. Sacrifice, personal or organizational, is deeply emotional; and it is an instinct that is earned through trial, difficult decisions, and the acquired ability to pioneer new paths.

Notes

1. Jane Levere, "After the 'Crying Indian', Keep America Beautiful Starts a New Campaign," *The New York Times*, July 16, 2013.

2. David J. Garrow, *Bearing the Cross: Martin Luther King Jr., and The Southern Christian Leadership Conference*. William Morrow & Co., November 1986.

3. Frederick Perls, *In and Out the Garbage Pail*. San Francisco: Gestalt Therapy Press, 1969.

4. Tom Perrotta, "Joe Flacco's Awesome Mediocrity," *Wall Street Journal*, December 11, 2016.

5. Russell Roberts, "Ode to the Patriots," *Wall Street Journal*, January 31, 2008.

6. The author of this book is neither a fan nor non-fan of the Patriots. He is a fan of the Dallas Cowboys who were once tribal but seem to have lost their way.

7. Marina Koren, "The Dark Saga of Katie Bouman," *The Atlantic*, April 15, 2019.

8. Carmine Gallo, "Steve Jobs, Get Rid of the Crappy Stuff," *Forbes*, May 16, 2011.

9. Andrew Roberts, *Napoleon: A Life*. Penguin Group, November 4, 2014.

10. H. J. Leavitt, H. J. "Applied Organisational Change in Industry: Structural, Technological and Humanistic Approaches." In J. G. March (Ed.), *Handbook of Organisation*. Chicago, IL: Rand McNally and Company, 1965.

11. Albert H. Segars, William Kettinger, and Warren Harkness, "Process Management and Supply-Chain Integration at the Bose Corporation," *Interfaces*, June 2001.

12. James Stavridis, "Growing Threats to the U.S. at Sea," *Wall Street Journal*, June 2, 2017.

13. Brian Costa and Jared Diamond, "Baseball's Comically Underpaid Young Stars," *Wall Street Journal*, March 8, 2016.

14. Ben Foldy, "The Minivan is Out of Style; Sales Fade as SUVs Gain Traction", *Wall Street Journal*, August 1, 1019.

· 9 ·

TRIBAL SPIRIT

I wish it to be remembered that I was the last man of my tribe to surrender my rifle.
— Sitting Bull

Hopefully, as you have explored the approach of "tribal innovation" through its defining instincts, you have recalled a few times in your life when you felt connected with a group of fellow adventurers on the quest for something ambitious. From the perspective of leadership, these instincts provide a testing ground for the predisposition of an organization to accomplish challenging or breakthrough projects. As a researcher, consultant, and academic, I have had the privilege of working with a variety of businesses, non-profits, and military organizations. I have also directed, participated in, and studied "super projects". Because of this, I have been asked, from time to time, about the "culture" or "secret ingredient" behind innovative organizations. In one instance, I was pressed by a very senior member of the United States military for a "one-sentence" answer to the question. I simply said, "It is tribal". Of course, that answer requires some definition and context and that is what led to this research and this book. However, along the way, I also observed a lot of initiatives and programs of innovation that masqueraded as tribal. They also masqueraded as innovative. The very ironic thing about these initiatives is that it was an organization that unwittingly killed innovation in the name of innovation. So, just to draw a contrast, and to have a little fun, let's take a look at the ways an organization can kill innovation. Nothing you read in the next section is in any way tribal. It is a humorous, yet true, counter demonstration.

Eight Innovative Ways to Kill Innovation

Creating a tribal mindset takes a lot of commitment and a lot of brave leadership. Leaders have to be willing to "unbundle" some roles and responsibilities that have been part of the mythical "messiah" model and entrust them to members of the tribe. You have to chase ambitious goals and you have to accept success where it is, not where you want it to be. To top it off, you must be willing to endure hardship and sacrifice. To be honest, that is asking an awful lot! In addition, there may be a deep state of non-tribal, obstructionist actors that are influential and wish to block any innovative effort or any change initiative. No wonder some organizations are not willing to take the leap. Therefore, instead of becoming tribal, they seek other ways to be innovative without "really" being innovative. Ironically, in walking this path, the programs of innovation they adopt not only stall innovation, they kill it. Yet, the optics suggest that the organization has embraced innovation. It is a win-win. The organization talks about innovation yet is ensuring that nothing innovative happens. No sacrifice is made, no hardship endured, and small ideas seem like big ideas. There are eight basic strategies to make this happen. They are illustrated in Figure 9.1 and discussed in the following sections.

Assign Innovation to a Czar or Committee

Rather than "bother" organizational members with the extra burden of thinking or acting innovatively, the load is passed to an "innovation czar" or an "innovation steering committee". This is an innovation trick invented in major universities that has been adopted by many other organizations. Higher education should apologize for the strategy; many ideas have been lost in its practice. The committee or czar is charged with fostering innovation within the organization. This is analogous to asking a clocksmith to replace several gears in a pocket watch with the stipulation that the clock continue to run during the repair and not lose a second of time, this is very difficult to accomplish and most likely beyond the skill and responsibility of a czar or steering

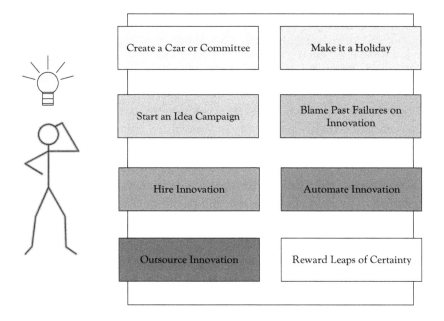

Figure 9.1: Eight Ways to Innovatively Kill Innovation

committee. The message to the organization is that the responsibility for innovation lies with someone else. In addition, the organization can appoint a czar or a committee that will make sure nothing innovative happens. They will also have no budget or authority. Therefore, you have an innovation committee, very good optics, but nothing "too" innovative will happen, the organization stays in its comfort zone. This is one of the best strategies for innovatively killing innovation. Now, to be fair, some organizations may find a chief innovation officer or steering committee to be useful in coordinating activities across a complex organization. However, the core of real innovation does not tend to live in these structures. Instead, it tends to be deep in the labs and inner workings that are beyond the vison of a steering committee. In the innovative organizations researched for this book, innovation was not culled out of the fabric and placed in a committee. Such a structure was seen as unneeded bureaucracy and something to be avoided. Should your organization be engaged in the practice, it is likely that you have lost some innovative ground. It is not the fault of the people, it is the structure of the arrangement and the subtle, yet powerful, negative message it sends to organizational members about their role and responsibility in driving innovation.

Idea Campaigns

I think we have all been greeted by a new leader with the words "*I have an open-door policy*". All I can think of when I hear this phrase is Yuck! I keep hoping that I will hear a new leader say, "*I hope you have an open-door policy, I will be by to see you*". That would be revolutionary, and it would be tribal. It is also something highly noticeable in innovative organizations. Everybody has an open door and there is a lot of visiting and being visited. However, if a leader wants to maintain the optics of innovation without acquiring a lot of visits and visiting, they will launch the idea campaign. Idea campaigns have several forms. The most obvious is the statement by a leader that goes like this, "If you have any ideas, please feel free to come by my office and let's chat". To be very cynical but honest, this is a clarion call to everyone that has a problem such as bad office location, no place to plug in their hybrid car, or not enough healthy choices in the vending machines. Not to belittle these issues but that is not innovation. Leaders will sometimes compound this phenomenon by creating electronic or physical suggestion boxes. These boxes will quickly fill up with complaints or small ideas. Because it is impossible to address all of the "ideas" that are forwarded, they go without acknowledgement which further erodes the sense of innovation and responsiveness. Finally, it is common for a leader to ask for your "game-changing ideas". This is the "idea lottery". By launching this initiative, a leader has asked organizational members for something that is typically beyond their capability. It is not a capability or creative issue. It is simply that game-changing ideas are elusive, tricky, and hard to describe and require a few minds. The notion that your idea might win the "idea lottery" is so appealing that many will try, but the odds of winning are incredibly low. This leads to frustration and disappointment. However, the end has been achieved. The organization appears to drive innovation when in fact innovation is being tortured to death.

Hire Innovation

Hiring innovation into the organization has great optics and the promise of immediate results. The most obvious way to achieve this is to hire a chief executive officer or a senior executive (or two) who have some background in innovation and who mention the word quite a bit during the interview process. Search firms can be very useful in this process. The idea is that the executive will "infect" the organization with their innovativeness. Suddenly, everyone will become more innovative and, as a result, organizational innovation is achieved. I have experienced this "firsthand" a few times. As good as the narrative "plays", and it can be successful, it sometimes does not go quite as expected.[1] The former CEO may have left a legacy that it is too hard to overcome. If they have stayed in the job too long, then talented people who might have ascended to the position or offered critical support have departed. Before their departure, the CEO may have staged a dramatic exit. Maybe an acquisition or strategic plan that makes it hard to find the new beginning. Perhaps the most significant obstacle is lack of "fit". Placing a visionary at the helm of an organization unwilling to change results in a costly old organization. Yet, this is the brilliance of the tactic. It then becomes very easy to place the blame on the new CEO and begin developing the narrative that we have "lost our way". Before long, order is restored, and a familiar and non-threatening face takes the helm. The same tactic can be used anywhere in an organization. Creative, boundary spanning, unique people are introduced to "shake the place up". The problem with this is the implicit message the tactic sends; the current collection of people, their ideas, motivation, and skills are not good enough. The organization needs a "kick in the pants". Also, from the first "town hall" meeting with the new CEO, an "us versus them" mentality begins to brew within the organization. This becomes even more amplified if the new CEO brings in a supporting cast to help move the change along. Again, any hope of building a shared vision and shared commitment to coming challenges is lost forever.

Outsource Innovation

Another great way to avoid the hard work of innovation is to outsource it to somebody else. There are a few ways to do this effectively. First, you can simply follow other innovators. Strategy consultants and academics call this "fast following."[2] The idea is to wait until you see someone innovate, then you copy or perhaps improve on the innovation. Proponents cite instances such as Apple in digital music, Google in digital navigation, and Facebook as examples.[3] In theory, you get all of the benefit and endure none of the risk. The problem is that even fast following involves some risk. *What if we follow the wrong lead? What if we follow and then want to turn back?* If an organization has resigned itself to following, then there is some evidence of risk avoidance. Questions such as these only heighten that predisposition. Therefore, it is probably more correct to view "fast followers" as real innovators and "fast following" as a nice idea but too risky for an organization lacking innovation. Plus, it builds a culture that is resigned to being, at best, a second-place finisher in ideas. This works against the instinct of ambition and perseverance. Nonetheless, it is a very effective way to look innovative without bearing the cost. Along with following, joint ventures, mergers, and consultants are great ways to outsource innovation. In these instances, the plan is to provide the bulk of muscle or expertise while the partner provides the bulk of vision and ideas. This can work but it is a very unbalanced partnership. Typically, idea makers have a real problem with monogamy and with sharing wealth.[4] Apple and AT&Ts partnership in the development of the iPhone is an example of this conundrum.[5] Although each partner has benefitted, Apple receives the accolades and rewards of the innovator while AT&T receives the scorn when network outages occur and the burden of being traded for another carrier. Outsourcing innovation to another organization is a very tempting way to seem innovative. However, it is not tribal. At best, the organization will reap the benefits of finishing behind the innovator. At worst it will reap the benefits of a participation trophy.

Make Innovation a Holiday

A great way to march under the innovation banner without being innovative is to make innovation a holiday. This is a very popular strategy for masquerading innovators. Typically, an event such as an "innovation summit" is staged in a very nice getaway location or the corporate learning center. Executives recall past stories about how the founder was "ahead of their time" in starting the company. Motivational speakers make guest appearances. There is a keynote speech along with food and wine. A facilitator will break the attendees into teams; they will then show them the IDEO shopping cart video. Armed with yellow stickies and the slogan "no idea is a bad idea", the innovation exercise is launched. The next day, they catch flights back to their home base and all is left behind at the summit. To be totally transparent, I have seen these firsthand and I have been a speaker on occasion. It is exhilarating to see the energy during the summit and disappointing to see it all left behind in the venue. This approach can work well to get lift off but you only get one shot at it. Once organizational members know that it is an "innovation show", then the energy and enthusiasm of participation drops considerably, no matter where the next summit is held. Another approach, and, yes, I have seen this a few times, is to declare this the year of innovation. Of course, the problem is that most everyone views this as putting up the hoopla of innovation for a year and then getting back to work as usual. Maybe next year will be the year of getting a decent pay raise. It is easy to laugh this one off, but if you think about it, everyone has seen something like this in action. Yearly innovation awards, innovation day, the random morning office meeting about innovation are all examples of innovation as an event rather than a tribal way of working. It is easier and has great optics, but it only lasts for the duration of the event.

Blame Innovation for Past Failure

A surefire way to kill innovation yet seem innovative is to blame innovation for past failure. In this case, the narrative is that the organization is too innovative and, as a result, some missteps took place. This is the cleverest of the strategies because it starts with the notion that the organization is a loaded gun of innovation. The challenge is to roll back some of that innovative spirit because it got us into trouble last time. I leaned on this strategy quite a bit in my younger days while explaining to my dad why his car, which I borrowed to attend an Aerosmith concert, was full of beer cans and smelled like pot. I told him I was being hyper-innovative. The strategy was a miserable failure for me. For organizations, this strategy really works if the narrative is about a different organization that suffered because of innovation. The story of the failure is told, and then there is some discussion about the "right" kind of innovation to pursue which typically means no innovation at all. Ironically, the conclusion becomes it is better not to be innovative. This is particularly dangerous because risk aversion tends to be a predisposition among individuals and organizations. This not only reinforces that notion, it also amplifies it by demonstrating a negative outcome of innovative behavior. It also assumes that the conditions that led to the failure are still in full effect. That said, the cleverness of the strategy is in the twist that frames doing "nothing innovative" as the most innovative thing that can be done. This strategy is brilliant, and when done properly it will guarantee innovative non-innovativeness. It is not tribal. It builds paranoia and a form of negative trust that will greatly inhibit the instincts of ambition, sacrifice, emergent structure, and navigation. Blaming something else for the lack of innovation is certainly not courageous. It stops all forward momentum and builds a sense that the organization is not in control of its destiny.

Automate Innovation

Organizations that are process minded are some of the most heralded in business literature. There is a discipline, ability to replicate, and certainty that goes along with "process". No doubt, it is a great characteristic and something worth chasing. However, it does open the door for innovative non-innovativeness. The temptation is to take innovation and turn it into a business process and automate it as much as possible. This means there is a process owner, a regimented way of executing the process, and lots of software support to help the process along. In fact, the more the technology can automate the process, the better. The argument goes that advanced technology provides simulation, virtual reality, artificial intelligence, data visualization, and a host of other capabilities that allow the organization to "standardize" innovation. In some sense, it is a high-tech version of outsourcing. The difference is that ideas enter the process and are then assessed and tested via technology and process specifications. The ideas are then sent back for revision or move to the next part of phase-gate process. There is a lot to like about this approach. It does highlight the importance of innovation. It is a formalized process with a clearly defined definition. It is possible to see the progress of an idea or project through digital technology. The technology can even become an idea generator.[6] However, the primary objective of automation is to lessen or eliminate the role of people. Hopefully, you have sensed how central the role of people is in a tribal approach to innovation. Therefore, technology may find its best use in a supporting role for innovation rather than in automating it. Creating a process and technological infrastructure for innovation does not create the deeper culture of innovation necessary for bigger ideas. In fact, it may be a catalyst for creating many incremental improvements that are not real innovations.[7] Yet, automating innovation through process and technology is an effective way to project innovation without really being innovative. In addition, it creates an "idea-making machine" that may not have the capacity or specifications to shape or process complex ideas. Therefore, it is fed only the ideas it can process which may be smaller versions of a bigger issue. The likely outcome is incremental improvement of that which already exists. Not necessarily a bad outcome, just not an innovative outcome.

Reward Leaps of Certainty

I was once asked by a former chief executive office who was considering an offer from a major university, *What is the most important skill for a university president?* It was a very easy question. I answered, *"Think small"*. I know you might think of that response as an indictment on university administrators. It is not, they are typically good people. The problem is that every incentive in a university hierarchy rewards small thinking. If your goal is to endure, then think small. Because of this, higher education administration attracts small thinkers and those that enter its ranks as big thinkers quickly learn to tone it down. Small thinking is not tribal thinking. Small thinking is focused on self-preservation, taking no chances, plausible deniability, delaying tough decisions, thinking about the next job. I believe this is why there is a bit of a crisis in university leadership.[8] However, the same type of phenomena is found in other organizations. The storyline goes this way: talk about innovation, promote it on the website, include it in the executive PowerPoint deck but only reward leaps of certainty. Again, the result is innovative non-innovativeness. If I have learned one thing in my career in business and in research, it is that people do exactly what they are provided incentive to do. Plus, "we the people" are quick to figure out the prevailing incentive. In many organizations, there is no incentive to broker new ways of doing things. In fact, the prevailing incentive system is to encourage keeping the status quo. Again, this rubs against the notion of being tribal. Knowledge flows become transactional rather than insightful. Navigation becomes systems of raw counts rather than logical chains of cause and effect. Risky projects are avoided, and no one is willing to sacrifice sacred cows for the emerging opportunity.

Again, these eight ways to innovatively kill innovation are meant to demonstrate the possible ways that organizations might attempt to sidestep the difficult task of building a culture that is tribal and has a strong predisposition for achieving bigger ambitions. The irony is that they work in the short term. However, imagine two competing organizations. Perhaps two business rivals or two sports rivals. One is tribal, each of the seven instincts is fully in place. The other depends on one or more of the eight innovative non-innovative approaches just described. It is easy to see that the tribal organization will likely come up with the most innovative path forward and also endure the longest. It is the secret behind the great sports teams, transformational movements in history, and the moment you achieved something you thought was out of reach. It is just a matter of finding that tribal spirit.

Finding Your Tribal Spirit

As a young boy of ten or eleven, I remember playing with toy race cars in the big family room while my father, his sisters, and my grandmother would talk about family business and everything else. I had no idea what they were talking about and I didn't care; it was a great time of my life, all I cared about were the race cars. On a Friday evening, while the talk was raging and my race cars were racing, one of my older cousins walked through the great family room on her way out for the evening. She was a stunning young woman and that night she chose a rather provocative outfit to wear. Along with the outfit, she had chosen quite a bit of make-up to wear just in case someone did not notice the outfit. I was amazed she was attempting to get past the gauntlet of her mother, grandmother, and two aunts in such attire. My aunts and grandmother were formidable, plus they had decided long ago it was not worth the effort to keep fit, wear fitted clothes, or do anything fashionable. Her mother, my aunt, stood up out of her chair, pointed at my cousin, and said, "*There is no way you are leaving this house looking like that! Get your behind back into your room and put on something decent.*" My other Aunt piled on, "*and wipe that war paint off of your face, you look cheap*". We were all stunned; the scene was dramatic. Then, my grandmother spoke; she said, "*Everybody shut the hell up! Let her shine her little light while she can. After all, we are where the parade is headed!*" I will never forget the look on my cousin's face. She ran back to her room and cried, not because of her clothes or of being called cheap but because of where she now knew the parade was headed! To complete the story, once she regained herself, she went out and shined her little light. She is also still a very stunning woman after all these years.

There are a few things to learn from that experience but the one most relevant for us is that finding tribal spirit is a matter of urgency. If we put it off or "kick the can down the road", the parade still marches on. If that parade is not innovative and not ambitious, it is easy to march along without realizing that time is wasting. Plus, we tend to get accomplished at marching to that pace and comfortable marching to that destination. The time to shine our little light is right now, not when it is too late. That little light is tribal spirit. Taking what has been discussed as tribal instincts and forging them into tribal spirit is as simple as envisioning a flaming arrow. Each part of the arrow represents something unique and important. Together, the parts of the arrow represent tribal spirit. This is illustrated in Figure 9.2.

The Feathering of Finding Your Way

The feathering of the flaming arrow symbolizes the tribal instincts of navigation as well as roles and responsibilities. Defining the purpose of an

Tribal Spirit

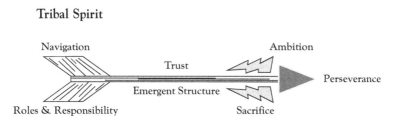

Figure 9.2: Tribal Spirit

organization and the role of everyone within that purpose is critical in acquiring and keeping the path. Too many times, this is described as developing a "strategy". It is more than that; it is developing the right combination of roles, people to fill the roles, a worthy destination, and a sense of fortitude when things get turned upside down. This makes it like a watch; all of the gears must turn and synchronize so that the correct time is displayed. When the watch is placed in a different time zone, it can be adjusted to show the correct time without replacing all the gears or completely rebuilding the watch. Plus, all of this happens very fast. I was taught that "strategy" preceded all of these things. However, experience and the research for this book have taught me that "strategy" typically describes these things after they have occurred. Not to knock strategy, it is something good, just not enough. It seems dangerous to lean entirely on a strategy to guide the flaming arrow. Instead, there seems to be an alignment between the organization and its destination that evolves and adjusts. It is the interplay between the people and their roles/responsibilities and the outcomes as acquired and chased through the chain of logic.

The Shaft of Connectedness

The shaft of the arrow represents the people of the organization. Of course, without a shaft, the arrow is useless. If the shaft is crooked or out of alignment, then the arrow does not fly freely through the air. The stress of the misalignment interferes with the flight and also renders the feathers useless. Perfect alignment is equal to organizational connectedness. This is built on the interplay of trust and positive emergent structure. Without trust, members seek to protect their own interests and, taken to an extreme, mistrust may be more rewarded than trust. Trust is manifest in strong flows of knowledge among individuals, groups, and tribes. Emergent structure should reinforce a culture of people working together and supporting each other along the journey. In other words, emergent structure should reinforce trust and vice versa. Strong codes of conduct and shared values serve to unite groups and create a feeling of *Esprit De Corps*. The shaft serves to hold the pieces of the flaming arrow together. It is critical, yet, its importance can easily be underestimated. The feather of navigation and the flame of ambition cannot function without a shaft that is true.

The Flame of the Journey

The flame of the arrow represents the journey. It is the fire of ambition in achieving something extraordinary. It is thinking bigger about the world around you. It is creatively asking "*What is possible?*" rather than asking "*What did we do last time?*" The flame also represents the burn of sacrifice. Individually, we all make sacrifices in our careers and lives. Even when it is the right thing to do, sacrifice leaves its mark. Yet, it can be a mark of achievement in overcoming the very innate instinct of self-preservation. When the objective is ambitious, the act of sacrifice is made easier. Medals of valor have been awarded, martyrs have found their place in history, and ordinary people have become extraordinary because the objective mattered. The flame represents the important interplay between ambition and sacrifice. If leaders want to ask more from the members of their organization, then the destination must be worth the sacrifice. Organizationally, this plays out in sacrificing old ideas to make room for the pursuit of new initiatives. Every organization has limited capacity. Deciding what is truly important is the trigger for unlocking the sacrifice needed for extraordinary commitment.

The Point of Perseverance

The arrowhead represents the perseverance needed to resist and overcome the elements and obstacles that impede the flight of the arrow. Any innovative imitative is likely to encounter "rough air" from time to time. There will be naysayers and those that cheerlead for the defeat of the initiative. That can actually be part of the magic if the effort is tribal. Maybe if there is an absence of resistance, then the idea is not big enough or the initiative is not truly innovative. I often leaned on this line of thinking when the most beautiful girls in high school turned me down for dances and the senior prom. For leaders, it is important to note that there are innovative ways to kill innovation.

I listed eight of these earlier in the chapter. Keep in mind, innovation is a wide frontier. It is not just building products, launching marketing campaigns, or thinking of a better strategy. Launching an initiative to create more diversity and inclusiveness is innovation. Workforce development is innovation. Creating more sustainable business practices is innovation. Building a system of compensation and benefits is innovation. There are multiple organizational initiatives that are innovative; we just do not treat them as such. Any of these initiatives can be killed if attempted through a committee, a holiday, a process, or by following the trail of others. It takes a tribal effort to be successful. No arrow flies with only an arrowhead and no arrow is useful without an arrowhead. Persistence, endurance, and patience are not the most fun aspects of innovation; but they may well be the most important. They keep the flame alive, keep the shaft true, and enable the feathers. Together, the parts of the flaming arrow illustrate the all-important tribal spirit that can guide us as individuals and guide us as part of a working organization. It is the special magic of modern innovation.

Concluding Thoughts

At some point in our lives, it is likely that all of us experienced a feeling of purpose and belonging that was more than just being a member of a "team". In all likelihood, that experience resulted in some outcome that was more than the ordinary. It is also likely that traditional systems of management, process, and incentives have taken away the opportunity to experience that same sense of accomplishment and belonging within the workplace. Luckily, within very innovative organizations, tribal instincts that set a more ambitious agenda, thirst for risky projects, overcome obstacles, and use value systems as an organizing principle are alive and well. These tribes are pioneering incredible breakthroughs in technology, chemistry, medicine, and manufacturing. My belief is that these organizations practice a form of modern management that is different and effective. Yet, it harkens back to the spirit and tribes of the past that were equally ambitious and radical for their time.

Importantly, there is nothing exclusive about tribes and tribal membership, there is a place for all who wish to accomplish more than the ordinary. The central theme of the seven instincts and tribal spirit is *unity*. The modern technology of Bluetooth is a great example of this notion. Harald Bluetooth was a Viking king of Denmark many centuries ago. Unlike other kings, Harald brought different Viking tribes together, uniting all of Scandinavia. The pioneer of Bluetooth technology, Jim Kardach, considered the technology to be about uniting; therefore, he decided to name the invention Bluetooth. In fact, the Bluetooth symbol blends the Nordic runes for 'B' and 'H', the initials of Harald Bluetooth.

Many of today's leaders are faced with innovation challenges that require the commitment, zeal, and dedication that is beyond a typical team. In addition, many of today's professionals are seeking something more meaningful in their work. A unique opportunity exists to unite these challenges with the interpersonal desire for connectedness through the building of tribes and adoption of tribal instincts. This book develops a set of principles and assorted tools for creating tribal spirit within the organizational frame that leads to a predisposition to accomplish more than the ordinary. In fact, it is a path for creating a context in which ordinary people accomplish extraordinary things. The accomplishments of the Wright Brothers, NASA's Mission Control during Apollo 13, the New England Patriots, Apple's MacIntosh Team, the 1980 USA Men's Hockey Team, the Zulus, Norseman, and the Lakota are just a few of the many examples that demonstrate what is possible within the context of a tribe. Capturing the instincts that defined these tribes within the context of today's workplace is the needed and elusive part of "innovative culture" that is necessary for capturing and chasing ideas that once seemed impossible. Tribal spirit is an amazing phenomenon. Like most things, it is tempting to say that it is something that must be seen to be believed. However, it is a bit more intricate than that; it is something that must be believed to be seen.

Notes

1. Jay Conger and David Nadler, "When CEOs Step Up to Fail," *Sloan Management Review*, April 15, 2004.
2. Scott D. Anthony, "First Mover of Fast Follower?" *Harvard Business Review*, June 14, 2012.
3. Shane Snow, *Smartcuts: How Hackers, Innovators, and Icons Accelerate Success*. HarperCollins, 2014.
4. Shayndi Raice and Yukari Iwatani Kane, "Verizon Finally Lands the iPhone," *Wall Street Journal*, January 8, 2011.
5. Laura M. Holson, "Even AT&T is Startled by the Cost of the iPhone Partnership," *The New York Times*, October 22, 2008.

6. Dan Solomon, "IBM's Watson Creates New Trailer for AI Thriller 'Morgan'," *Fast Company*, August 31, 2016.

7. Leslie Kwoh, "You Call That Innovation?" *Wall Street Journal*, May 23, 2012.

8. Douglas Belkin, "No Confidence: College Faculties Rebel with More Votes Against Leadership," *Wall Street Journal*, May 19, 2018.

APPENDIX—THE SUPER PROJECTS

Event Horizon Telescope

The EHT is an international collaboration of computer scientists, physicists, astronomers, mathematicians, and engineers that have created a computational telescope by uniting the technology of eight observatories around the world and integrating the expertise of well-focused research teams. The expertise and roles of the globally located teams consist of instrumentation, data processing, data analysis, simulation, and multi-wave science, as well as engineering and computer programming. Each telescope within the network works in concert and is coordinated through extremely precise atomic clocks. Through the use of artificial intelligence and other computer algorithms, the images collected throughout the network are reconciled to create an image of the black hole at the center of our universe. They realized this incredible objective in April 2019.[1] The image that was captured provided physical evidence of Einstein's theories of relativity and also gave the world a glimpse of something that was once thought to be forever invisible.

MIT's Broad Institute

MIT's Broad Institute is pioneering the field of disease prevention through analysis and mapping as well as engineering of the human genome. The institute was founded to seize the opportunity that arose from the Human Genome Project—the international effort that successfully deciphered the entire human genetic code. To gain a comprehensive view of the human genome and biological systems, the institute integrates the works of many laboratories. This means working in nimble teams that combine biology, chemistry, mathematics, computation, and engineering with medical science and clinical research. The institution fosters an atmosphere of creativity, risk-taking, and open sharing of data and research. Broad Institute is an "experiment" in a new way of doing science. It spans some of Boston's leading institutions (Harvard, MIT, and Harvard-affiliated hospitals) and scientific disciplines (biology, chemistry, medicine, computer science, and engineering). The Broad community includes more than three thousand scientists, committed to advancing research in areas including infectious disease, cancer, psychiatric research, and cardiovascular disease.

India's Mars Orbiter

In India, the Mars Orbiter Mission, also known as Mangalyaan, is an astounding testimony of efficiency and advanced engineering.[2] The Mars Orbiter Mission probe lifted-off from the First Launch Pad at Satish Dhawan Space Centre (Sriharikota Range SHAR), Andhra Pradesh, using a Polar Satellite Launch Vehicle (PSLV) on 5 November 2013. The MOM probe spent about a month in the Earth orbit, where it made a series of seven apogee-raising orbital maneuvers before trans-Mars injection on 30 November 2013. After a 298-day transit to Mars, it was inserted into the Mars orbit on 24 September 2014. The primary objective of the mission is to develop the technologies required for designing, planning, management, and operations of an interplanetary mission. The secondary objective is to explore Mars' surface features, morphology, mineralogy, and Martian atmosphere using indigenous scientific instruments. The Mars Orbiter Mission team won US-based National Space Society's 2015 Space Pioneer Award in the science and engineering category. Nearly half of all attempted missions to Mars have failed, however; India became the first country to put a spacecraft in orbit around another planet on its first try. In addition, India accomplished this feat on a tiny budget: 4.5 billion rupees, or U.S. $73 million—less than the budget of science fiction blockbusters like *The Martian* or *Gravity*. The spacecraft is in an elliptical orbit with a high apoapsis where, with its high-resolution camera, it is taking full-disk color imagery of Mars.

Cal Tech's Space Solar Power Project

At Cal Tech, the Space Solar Power Project is pioneering the concept of capturing solar power in space and wirelessly transmitting it back to Earth. This initiative is already delivering promising results and could become a limitless source of energy in the future.[3] The concept is based on the modular assembly of ultralight, foldable, 2D integrated elements. Integration of solar power and RF conversion in one element avoids a power distribution network throughout the structure, further reducing weight and complexity. This concept enables scalability and mitigates a local element failure impact on other parts of the system. Their research solves the fundamental challenges associated with implementing space solar by integrating ultralight and shape accurate structures with high-efficiency photovoltaics and large-scale phased array power transmission into a two-dimensional scalable, deployable spacecraft.

Korea's Robot Research Initiative

The Robot Research Initiative (RRI) in Korea is a pioneering and very productive collaboration between the government and industry giants such as Samsung and Hyundai in the development of advanced robotics. RRI is currently a leading institute in the medical robotics field, especially in the area of biomedical micro/nano-robotics. RRI is one of the largest institutions among university robotics laboratories in Korea and competes globally. Robot Research Initiative created the world's first colonoscopy robot in 2001 and the world's first intravascular micro-robot for the treatment of blood vessel–related diseases in 2010. In March 2015, the center developed an active capsule endoscope and has signed a 1 billion won contract to transfer the technology to Woo Young Medical, a medical device manufacturer. Under the contract, the center will receive two percent of endoscope sales as a licensing fee.

Open AI

Open AI began as a non-profit artificial intelligence research company. Their goal is to advance digital intelligence in the way that is most likely to benefit humanity as a whole. Unconstrained by a need to generate financial return, Open AI can better focus on their objective and produce science in the vein of research universities or government sponsored "think tanks". The organization aims to "freely collaborate" with other institutions and researchers by making its patents and research open to the public. Microsoft recently invested $1 billion in Open AI to enhance its Azure cloud-computing platform. The companies said they would jointly develop supercomputing technologies for Azure.

New Horizons (NASA)

New Horizons is a NASA mission to study the dwarf planet Pluto, its moons, and other objects in the Kuiper Belt, a region of the solar system that extends from about 30 AU, near the orbit of Neptune, to about 50 AU from the Sun. It was the first mission in NASA's New Frontiers program, a medium-class, competitively selected and principal investigator-led series of missions. (The program also includes Juno and OSIRIS-REx.) New Horizons was the first spacecraft to encounter Pluto, a relic from the formation of the solar system. By the time it reached the Pluto system, the spacecraft had traveled farther away and for a longer time period (more than nine years) than any previous deep space spacecraft ever launched.

Berkeley Lab

Berkeley Lab is a multiprogram science lab in the national laboratory system supported by the U.S. Department of Energy through its Office of Science. It is managed by the University of California and is charged with conducting unclassified research across a wide range of scientific disciplines. Technologies developed at Berkeley Lab have generated billions of dollars in revenues and thousands of jobs. Berkeley Lab was founded by Ernest Orlando Lawrence, a UC Berkeley physicist who won the 1939 Nobel Prize in physics for his invention of the cyclotron, a circular particle accelerator that opened the door to high-energy physics. It was Lawrence's belief that scientific research is best done through teams of individuals with different fields of expertise, working together. His "team science" concept is a Berkeley Lab legacy

Defense Advance Research Projects Agency (DARPA)

The Defense Advanced Research Projects Agency (DARPA) is an agency of the United States Department of Defense responsible for the development of emerging technologies for use by the military. The genesis of that mission and of DARPA itself dates to the launch of Sputnik in 1957, and a commitment by the United States that, from that time forward, it would be the initiator and not the victim of strategic technological surprises. Working with innovators inside and outside of government, DARPA has repeatedly delivered on that mission, transforming revolutionary concepts and even seeming impossibilities into practical capabilities. The ultimate results have included not only game-changing military capabilities such as precision weapons and stealth technology, but also such icons of modern civilian society such as the Internet, automated voice recognition and language translation, and Global Positioning System receivers small enough to embed in myriad consumer devices.

Notes

1. "Scientists Release First Image of a Black Hole," *Wall Street Journal*, April 12, 2019.
2. "Why India's Mars mission is so cheap—and thrilling," *BBC News*, September 24, 2014.
3. "Solar Power Stations in Space Could Supply the World with Limitless Energy," *Forbes*, March 12, 2018.

Lightning Source UK Ltd.
Milton Keynes UK
UKHW021357070722
405523UK00004B/91